To
Walter

Keep believing that the best
is yet to come... it is.

Have a Great Forever!!

Warmest regards,
Vince Pesce
☺

Renaissance Selling
ENDURING WISDOM FROM THE ITALIAN MASTERS

By
Vince Pesce

What Others Are Saying About *Renaissance Selling*:

"I thought books on selling skills would help one drift off to sleep, not keep them up all night! I found it easier to retain more of the book's instructional message through the clever use of the story format."
>   Don Dutson, Jr.
>   "Fabric Merchant in Training" and
>   President, Fabrics Direct, Inc.

"I found myself making notes and planning how we could use these key points from the Chronicles. A very exceptional book that is filled with ideas stressing high character, ethics, professionalism and especially the importance of having God be a part of your business life."
>   John Bridgman
>   President, ABB Control Inc.

"Timeless truths ... If every salesperson lived by Vince's Chronicles, the business world would be revolutionized. Renaissance Selling is a winning philosophy that all sales people should embrace."
>   Dick Biggs, author of
>   *If Life Is A Balancing Act, Why Am I So Darn Clumsy?*

"What a way to weave a story! I never thought a "rag peddler" could teach so much. I'm looking forward to expanding our group into a renaissance way of thinking."
>   D. M. Duncan Jr.
>   Senior Vice President, Sales and Marketing
>   Peachtree Fabrics, Inc.

"Renaissance Selling is both entertaining and informative, coupled with a spirit of enthusiasm for professional selling. It captures the fundamental principles of salesmanship that lead to a long-term, trusting relationship between the seller and buyer."
>   Julian V. Pittman
>   President, ARTRAC Company

"'I found that the Chronicles and the Salesperson's Credo alone make up a complete sales training program. A must have for any serious sales professional. Vince's book is worth its weight in gold.
>   William M. Karszes, Ph.D.
>   President, Plastic Associates, Inc.

Renaissance Selling

ENDURING WISDOM FROM THE ITALIAN MASTERS

By

Vince Pesce

Published by

Fish Publishing
P.O. Box 450093
Atlanta, Georgia 31145-0093

Library of Congress Catalog Card Number: 95-90608

Pesce, Vince
RENAISSANCE SELLING:
Enduring Wisdom From The Italian Masters

ISBN 1-887951-11-3

1. Selling
2. Small Business
3. Business
4. Self-Improvement

Printed in the United States of America

Dedication

To My Grandparents. They left Italy from the ports in Genoa and Naples in the late eighteen hundreds and arrived at Ellis Island in the New York Harbor. They left family and friends to look for a better life. They found it.

To My Parents. They taught my sister Catherine and me the importance of love of God and love of family. By their lives, they demonstrated pride, integrity, and the importance of always looking for the bright side. They first introduced me to the importance of self-motivation.

To My Children, Marie Angela and Vincent (Vince) J. III. They are renaissance people of the "Now" generation. They have influenced me as much as I hope I have influenced them. They have taught me the value of patience and looking at things from a different angle. I hope that I have showed them the importance of love of God, love of others, and love of self.

To Almighty God. His blessings and guidance continually provide the strength that lead me to feel that the best is yet to come. I believe and know it is!

Renaissance

ren•ais•sance (rénisans) n. [Fr. renaitre, to be born anew] 1. a new birth; rebirth; revival 2. the great revival of art, literature, and learning in Europe in the 14th, 15th, and 16th centuries, based on classical sources: it began in Italy and gradually spread to other countries and marked the transition from the medieval world to the modern.

— Webster's New World Dictionary

The gender references used in this story reflect the culture of the renaissance period.

Acknowledgments

This book is written in appreciation of the thousands of salespeople who have passed my way. Their influence, along with the numerous executives whom I have served as a trainer, consultant and public speaker, convinces me that success in sales comes to those who have what are broadly identified as "the right attitudes."

I also want to thank the hundreds of prospects and customers I have had the privilege of calling on, and serving, in the last thirty years. May the next thirty be just as exciting. If I was unable to convince you to buy from me the last time, how about giving me another chance now?

Putting this book together could not have been completed without the help of many contributors. I am deeply grateful for their assistance. They are: Greg McCabe; Vic Mazza, his daughter Denise, and all the Mazzas who have encouraged me on this project; David Wishart, who helped in the initial layout; and David Bernardy, who provided very valuable input in the editing phase as well as the chapter illustrations. A special note of gratitude to my buddy, John Fullerton, who gave up part of two vacations to help complete this project. God bless him and his family. Also my cousin, John Corbani, who provided valuable suggestions—he has not lost his touch! The final editing could not have been completed without the impassioned support of Carole Rucinski and Catherine Manning. I thank you all and I love you all.

Preface

As a sales apprentice right out of engineering school, I attempted to put the selling process in a logical sequence. While looking for a simple formula to duplicate, I quickly discovered that there was not a magical approach that always resulted in a successful contact, presentation and order. It became apparent that if selling was that predictable, everyone in the profession would be successful. They are not.

Although there are steps that always had to be taken, the results were not always positive. That is when I realized that selling is part science and part art. Most of the science contribution relates to your products, services and other knowledge you must have. That, plus the sales skills necessary to convey what you know, are essential basics. They are the admission price you must pay. Many books have been written on professional salesmanship skills, including my best seller published by Prentice Hall, *A Complete Manual of Professional Selling.*

When you realize that some individuals have read every book on sales techniques they can get their hands on, attended every seminar and sales rally possible and still are not successful, you understand that success does not come from just having knowledge and sales skills. There is also an artistic quality to sales that must be mastered. By "artistic," I mean characteristics such as creativity, innovation, motivation, and self-discipline. Basically, I am speaking of the attitudes that a successful salesperson must have. Proper attitudes make the engine go in salespeople.

Thousands of program participants, recognizing the importance of the right attitudes, have suggested I write this book. I agreed, while advising that real, personal, long-term motivation and growth will not come from a book— this or any book. A person's success will be in direct proportion to his self-motivation—the "Ya Gotta Wanna" factor. We must first want to do better tomorrow than today, then take positive action to make it happen.

Renaissance Selling is a book of proven, time-tested sales attitudes. It conveys the essence of over 1,200 of my sales training and motivational programs for some of the finest companies and trade associations in the world. If you follow its principles, you will sell more.

I selected the title and format for this book because it gave me an opportunity to briefly comment on a very exciting period in the arts and sciences. The Renaissance originated in Italy and spread to the rest of Europe during the period from 1400 to 1550 A.D. Renaissance means a revival, a rebirth.

If you are not doing some of the things that our principal character, Giuseppe Pesce, learned to do, perhaps you need a renaissance experience in your life. Enjoy the book and continued success.

Vince Pesce

Table of Contents

An Order Form is in the back of this book for your convenience.

Introduction

My name is Giuseppe Pesce, some call me Pepe. I sell fabrics for the House of Pesce, my family's business, and I am continually striving to become better at my craft. Selling has not always been easy for me. Even now, I know that I must always strive to keep my skills sharp and my attitude right.

My efforts improved after I started to apply the proven principles of success told to me by those who helped in my training. This book is about those principles. If they can help me sell more, I am sure they will help you.

I was nineteen when I started traveling in a sales territory in the early fifteen hundreds, and I still work for my grandfather, Vincenzo Giuseppe Pesce, the patriarch of the House of Pesce, the largest decorative fabrics purveyor in all of *Italia*, maybe in the whole world. Grandfather's business started and flourished during the Italian Renaissance. He was, and still is, my guiding light, my sales trainer, my confidant, my mentor.

This story starts upon my return from a very disappointing week of traveling as a sales apprentice attempting to sell in the territory. I did not think that I could ever sell and was extremely frustrated and ready to quit. *Papa*, which I lovingly call my grandfather, recognized the situation and said we should start a comprehensive training program to show me the essential skills and attitudes necessary for success in sales.

This story is about my salesmanship training program and the influence that Grandfather and others had in my development. These influential people are the masters of Italy—the Italian Masters, who are the artists, writers, and scholars, as well as the leaders in commerce, politics and religion. They are all involved in the great rebirth of the culture some are calling the Italian Renaissance. I believe the salesmanship truths and principles the Italian Masters passed on to me are timeless. They will be as valid in the years to come as they are today. As long as people buy from people, these ideas, when applied consistently, will help anyone sell more.

Giuseppe Pesce

CHAPTER 1

My Return From a Week in the Territory

Recognizing that Improvements are Required

The wagon creaked softly as I approached my home late one Friday night. As I got closer, I urged the horse off the road, avoiding the holes and rocks, and onto the grass pasture. I tried to move quietly. Although I had been out for the whole week, the wagon was still almost full of bolts of fabric. When the wagon is light, it does not bounce as hard, and it makes less noise. I wished I had sold more!

Grandfather and grandmother lived next to our home, and I was sure they would be listening for my wagon. They always did. I wished they could not hear me that night. I had a terrible week in the territory. Off the road and on the grass, I led the horse to our barn. I knew *Mama-mia* would be waiting to see me with something on the hearth for dinner. I must have been thinking more about dinner than leading the horse, because I suddenly heard a loud *snap!* and the cart leaned towards one side. "Great, I thought, a classic ending to a terrible week, few sales, and now a broken axle."

It was always a joy to see Mama. We hugged, and she asked, "How is my sweet son Giuseppe? I see you walked the horse through the pasture, did you have a poor week as a sales apprentice in the territory?"

"Mama, I am fine, *grazie*. How can you tell I had a poor week? Does it show on my face? Is it so obvious?"

"Pepe, my baby, it is not in your face, but you know since you were a little baby, you could never keep a secret from me. Also, I remember when your father first started out traveling in the territory as a sales apprentice. When he returned, I could tell by the step of the horse and how high the wagon stood above the axle if the wagon was heavy or light. Also, my baby, when he did not want grandfather to hear, he would lead the horse on the grassy pastures, just like you did coming in. Pepe, did you send any pigeons?"

"No, *Mama mia*, not one pigeon."

Mother was referring to the homing pigeons used to send in orders from customers in the territory. A narrow strip of leather with the fabric requirements written on it was tied to the pigeon's leg, and it was released. In a few hours or less, it would arrive at our facility in Florence. The order would be prepared and sent out on the next wagon.

"Mama, I do not think I can ever be a successful sales master and walk in my father's place, and I know Grandfather is relying on me very heavily. I wish father was still alive."

"So do I, my son, so do I."

My father had died from a sudden fever while working in the territory last year. At times like this, when his wisdom would have been so invaluable, I missed him most.

"Pepe, you will learn, and you will do very well as a sales apprentice for the House of Pesce. You will become a sales master like your father, Vincenzo. Both your father and grandfather knew of your potential when they spoke of your talents.

"Tomorrow, you will meet with grandfather and ask him for his assistance. He faced the same tough situations that you now face when he started out into the territory. Your father, who ultimately sold more than Papa, did not reach his stride until he was in the territory quite a while. You will do very well, my baby."

"Mother, with Father and Grandfather successful as sales masters, why am I not doing better?"

"My baby, being born into a family of peddlers does not automatically assure you of being successful. It takes practice and training to become a sales master. I feel it in my heart—you will do better than both your father and your grandfather. You also will become a sales master. Pepe, you know the fabric business. You grew up and learned about materials, cutting patterns and designs. They are valuable traits of the sales master. Do you agree?"

Being born into a family of peddlers does not automatically assure you of being successful. It takes practice and training to become a sales master.

"*Si*, Mama. It seems that I have been in training for a long time."

"Giuseppe, I frequently heard your father talk about three areas for success as a sales master. He said they were all related. First, there is the knowledge you must have about the business. Then there are the selling skills you acquire that help when you talk to customers. These are tied together with all the necessary attitudes, including desire and drive. You have an excellent start, and your grandfather will help you complete your training. Pepe, because you are passionate about being a sales master, you will become one. Now come, have a nice dinner, and things will seem much brighter tomorrow. You will see. I have prepared one of your favorite dishes, pasta primavera. It is hot on the fire. I made it with fresh pasta and vegetables from the garden. I simmered the peppers, cauliflower, onions, and broccoli in olive oil and garlic before adding my crushed tomatoes. I cut the pasta in fettuccine strips. Sit down— eat. You will enjoy it. Your sister, Maria Angela, had a wonderful bowl for dinner and then took a crock to the theater for Vincenzo. Your brother is in rehearsals for tomorrow's show. Eat now—your grandfather will teach you."

> ౧ళ౨
> *If attitude and passion for selling are important, then I was sure I would become a sales master.*
> ౧ళ౨

Before I went to bed, I wrote in my territory log what Mama had said about knowing as much as I can about the fabrics business and learning the skills to talk to customers. I wanted to remember Mama's comments about the attitude and passion required for success as a sales master. I promised myself to strive to reach the high achievements of my father and the plans of my grandfather. If attitude and passion for selling are important, then I was sure I would become a sales master. I slept well.

CHAPTER 2

The Saturday Sales Meeting

The Need for Sales Training

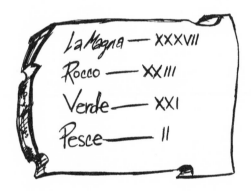

La Magna — XXXVII

Rocco — XXIII

Verde — XXI

Pesce — II

As was Grandfather's practice, every Saturday morning he asked all the territory salesman to come into the facility with their wagons. It was an ideal time to restock the wagons for the next week's trip, make any repairs or required maintenance on the wagons and meet with the salesmen. He also wanted to review the sales activities of the week. The purpose was not necessarily to compare the performance of one salesman versus another, but to help Grandfather and his chief accountant, *Signore* Enrico Santucci, to determine what was sold. *Signore* Santucci had a brother who was a Rabbi, but that is a story for later.

My sister, Marie Angela, and *Signore* Santucci typically conducted the meeting, with Grandfather sitting on the side and commenting as required. My sales performance was the worst of all the salesmen, even the other sales apprentices.

Marie Angela kept records on a large slate of black marble with a piece of soft stone. Next to each salesman's name, she wrote the total number of bolts of fabric sold, both from the wagon and by pigeon. Also, because Grandfather wanted to evaluate his pigeon delivery system, we recorded the number of orders that were received "by air," as he liked to say.

During the meeting, Grandfather would mention any new fabrics we had received during the week, and identify any complaints from the customers. This also was his opportunity to give us a little inspirational message. That Saturday he talked about striving to do better each day and not being discouraged if you have a poor experience with one merchant. "Just try again with the next customer," was his advice.

With my poor results staring me in the face, and all the other salesmen having much better numbers, I really could not concentrate on his message. I stared into space and wondered if I should stay in Grandfather's business or try another career. Maybe I could go into law like Uncle Giovanni, or into the arts like my brother Vincenzo. There was a lot to think about.

I am sure Grandfather saw my blank stare during the meeting, because he made certain to get my attention and ask me to stay after the others left.

Putting his arms on my shoulder he said, "My Giuseppe, son of my son, I see by your demeanor that you are not in the best of spirits." He did not wait for my response. I guess he could read my face pretty clearly. My sales results said it all.

"In selling, there are periods when you may not get the results you desire, and you can very easily become discouraged. This discouragement, providing it is only temporary, is quite normal. Your father and I both experienced this reaction. All salespeople, from time to time, may become discouraged. It provides a platform to plan for improvements. If one is not aware of the low ground, then how can one appreciate the top of the hill? Do you feel discouraged right now, my Pepe?"

"Yes, Grandfather. Last week was not a very good one. I did not sell many bolts of fabric. I did not send home any pigeons. I do not feel that I have represented myself very well, nor have I helped the House of Pesce grow. My inexperience really showed this week, Grandfather."

"My son, my son, do not worry about the House of Pesce. It will survive, and someday, when I retire, you will be in the position of authority. The disappointments you experienced this week calling on merchants in the outer regions are no different than those experienced by other peddler salesmen, myself included. They are normal. When I started in business over thirty years ago, and first went out in the territory presenting our fabrics, I frequently slept in the wagon and cried myself to sleep moaning, 'How will I ever support my family?' There was Grandma, Uncle Giovanni and your father to think about. My mind would wander. Maybe there was another business I should have entered. Maybe I should go into the business of my father and his father before him. Maybe, like them, I should build docks. Maybe I should move the family back to the Island of Ischia. Many doubts went through my mind back then.

> ⟨ঞ⟩
> *Merchants to whom I presented my fabrics did not know the quality, they did not know who I was, and surely most of them did not know who, or what, the House of Pesce was.*
> ⟨ঞ⟩

"Pepe, some days I did not sell even one bolt of fabric. Merchants to whom I presented my fabrics did not know the quality, they did not know who I was, and surely most of them did not know who, or what, the House of Pesce was. Some joked, asking if I sold fresh fish." This last comment brought a smile to my face. I knew Grandfather was trying to cheer me up.

"Possibly the best sales master I ever saw was your father Vincenzo, may he rest in peace. If he had not been taken from us so suddenly, he would have trained you in the vital steps of how to become a sales master, a true professional salesperson. Unfortunately, God had a purpose for him and took him from us before his time. Now, it has become necessary to send you into the territory before you are fully prepared. I know you do not have the necessary training. You are only nineteen, and I am already expecting you to produce like one with much more training and experience. I made a mistake. I am sorry, my Giuseppe. Would you accept my deep apologies? You know

Grandfather wants only the best for you."

I was silent. I did not have to speak. I just hugged Grandfather and started crying. Tears flowed down my cheeks. Big tears were falling on the gold embroidered fish in a circle symbol on Grandfather's tunic. Papa held me very closely. I knew he hurt as deeply as I did.

"Oh, Grandfather, *Nonno*, I want so badly to be a successful sales apprentice. I want to become a sales master. Please show me how."

"I will, my son, I will," he responded. We both tried to compose ourselves as Grandfather stood up. "Pepe, next week you will start on a thorough sales apprentice training program. I will cut your travel time in the territory and spend more time with you. You will visit some local merchants, and I will have you talk to others who can help you learn about the exciting and sometimes frustrating activities that we call selling. We will all strive to help you learn what it takes to be a successful sales master. I pray that this is acceptable to you, my Pepe."

> ೮ঙ৩
> *All people who aspire to reach professional levels in sales, and other business activities, experience discouragement from time to time. It is not unusual.*
> ೮ঙ৩

I nodded.

"One thing, Pepe, before we start. Please remember that all people who aspire to reach professional levels in sales, and in other business activities, experience discouragement from time to time. It is not unusual."

"Why?" I asked.

"Well, to be successful, you must have or develop strong emotional feelings and a positive business sense. You must be able to relate to the people you sell to. You must have a high degree of simpatico with those you deal with. And because salesmen have these strong feelings, they are sometimes emotionally hurt when the person they are dealing with does not respond favorably. It is not unusual for you to be emotionally down after a rejection. You must look at a rejection as a sign to improve in a particular area."

"Grandfather," I asked, "please explain how to handle rejections, because that is when I become discouraged the most."

"Giuseppe, you must start by never taking any rejection personally. You must consider all rejections as a professional short-coming; that is, you did not perform as professionally as required to convince the person to buy from you. There was, at least in that circumstance, a void in what you did or did not do. Your professional shortcoming was rejected, not you. Learn from each rejection as you grow, and they will become fewer and farther between. Dealing with rejection is part of the 'rights of passage' for growing as a sales master. You must get over a rejection with one customer quickly. If you cannot get yourself emotionally prepared for the next stop, you may very easily lose that sale also before you even enter the shop."

I finally got a few words in . . . "Lose *before* I enter a shop? *Nonno*, how can that be?"

"Giuseppe, although we typically obtain an order after we visit a merchant, the really confident, experienced salesperson enters with the positive anticipation of getting the order. You start getting that order the minute you get off the wagon. You must see in your mind's eye that you will be successful."

"You enter the customer's place of business confidently, looking for opportunities to demonstrate how the merchant can grow his business, and satisfy more of his patrons with fabrics from the House of Pesce. You reflect in your smile, demeanor and approach that you are a sincere, honorable person. Your appearance shows that you are a professional and that you are there to service him and his patrons. Giuseppe, once the merchant feels comfortable with you, believes in what you say, and believes you are there to help him sell more of his merchandise, he will buy from you."

> ∞
> *You must start by never taking any rejection personally. You must consider all rejections as a professional shortcoming; that is, you did not perform as professionally as required to convince the person to buy from you.*
> ∞

"But, Pepe, the hour is getting late. Let us stop our training for today. Over the next couple of months, we will cover more of the proper steps to take as a successful sales master. When I sent you into the territory unprepared, I made a big mistake. Please accept my apologies. Your training really should have preceded your going out by yourself. I am looking forward, little Pepe, to helping you on your journey to becoming a sales master, the best ever to represent the House of Pesce. Are you ready to take the journey, starting now?"

"*Si*, Grandfather, I am ready. I cannot wait to learn as much as I can on how to be successful as a salesman. I believe I can become the greatest sales master in the territory. With your help and the grace of God, I know I can do it."

"Pepe, I am pleased you recognize the importance of having God's help as you proceed on your journey to become a sales master. I seek His guidance every day. When I started the business many years ago, I selected the fish inside a circle for our company's sign. The fish, a *pesce*, is a Christian symbol. The circle represents the world that God is the Lord over. Indeed, God has blessed this business. Do you agree, my grandson?"

"*Si*, Grandfather, God does bless and watch over us and all those who believe in Him."

"*Bene*, good. Now, Giuseppe, go home. Tell your mama about our discussion. Then you rest and enjoy the day with your family. Tomorrow, after church services, we will continue our discussions. Next week we start your salesmanship training. Tonight we are going to the theater. "

That evening the entire family was planning to go to the theater. We would see my little brother, Vincenzo, and his song and dance troupe perform. It was a special production. Grandfather, as a patron, had a special box. For now, I would forget my shortcomings as a sales apprentice and enjoy the evening.

CHAPTER 3

The Pesces Go to the Theater

Learning from Everyone We Meet

That night was the opening performance of Vincenzo's dance company. They had been practicing for weeks, and every time my baby brother came home he told us about how the show was getting better and better with each rehearsal. He was exhausted every night.

There was excitement and growing anticipation in the *teatro* as the usher showed us to our seats. Two things were very obvious. First, there was a very pleasant floral scent emanating from the burning lanterns, and second, no smoke was coming from them! Not only was the light brighter, I had never, before that day, seen a candle that did not emit a black wisp of smoke. When I later asked Uncle Giovanni about these special lanterns, he said that one of the professors at the university had been given a grant to invent a fluid or candle that would not emit black smoke when lit.

Uncle said that the Lorenzo de Medici family and other patrons of the arts, including Grandfather, became concerned about the many valuable paintings, tapestries and frescos in churches and museums that might be ruined if a smokeless lantern or candle were not invented soon. Uncle said that the lantern fluid being used that night was very difficult to make because it required special distillation equipment.

After the formulation was acceptable, they had to obtain the services of one of the finest glass blowers in all of Italy to make the distilling tubing and containers. The process worked because two professions—one of chemistry and science, and the other in the art of glass blowing—combined talents to solve the problem. The invention of the smokeless fluid was typical of the explosion of scientific, cultural and artistic activities going on in Florence. It was exciting.

As is Uncle Giovanni's way, when you ask him a question he not only gives you the answer, he goes through a brief history lesson and tells you the circumstances that surround the situation. That was his monastic and legal training. My brother, my sister and I frequently joked among ourselves that before you ask Uncle Giovanni a question, make sure you have the rest of the afternoon available to get the answer.

Uncle Giovanni continued with the story of the smokeless fluid: "The inventor found a combination of fish liver oils and olive oils that burned well without the black smoke when mixed with paraffin wax. Unfortunately, the burning mixture emitted a foul odor. By adding a mixture of inexpensive fluid made from eucalyptuses, anise and rose petals, the scent became very acceptable." In fact, it was pleasant. The results that night in the *teatro* were outstanding.

Grandfather had a special area reserved for us at the *teatro*. All patrons were given priority seating locations based on the size of their contribution. Grandfather and the House of Pesce were big donors. He was the second largest patron of the arts in Florence. He contributed money and fabrics for the curtains, flags, stage bunting and, of course, for the beautiful costumes. Our seats were in a small roped-off area, up front near the stage, slightly to the side and elevated. They are called boxes for some reason. Our view of the stage was excellent.

The theater was only two years old and the latest in technical and architectural design. The ceiling expanse, over 122 meters, had special roof trusses, making it the largest unsupported expanse ever built. It was designed by our own local engineer and architect, Leonardo da Vinci, and built by the craftsmen from Giovanni Corbani's business. It was said that Leonardo was also a brilliant sculptor and artist, a true genius. It was common knowledge that he had recently been commissioned by the Papacy to design a new church for Milano that would be almost twice the size of the *teatro*.

In our box were Grandfather and Grandmother, Uncle Giovanni and his wife, Aunt Catherine, my mother, my sister Marie Angela, and *Monsignore* Mazza. Also joining us were my grandparents' favorite personal and business friends, *Signore* and *Signora* Bugatti, and *Signore* and *Signora* Mandaro. *Signore* Bugatti was one of the largest merchants in Florence and the biggest customer of the House of Pesce. Grandfather considered his advice on business matters very important. The Bugattis had known my grandparents and my family for over thirty years. He was one of Grandfather's first customers. The Mandaros were long-time friends of the family.

For the show, Marie Angela had spent most of the day combing her hair and putting on fine perfume and cosmetics. *Zia* Catherine had made a special dress for her to wear this evening. It was made from the new silk fabric Grandfather had just received from China. Marie Angela looked beautiful in the dress. I suspected she was trying to catch the eye of Michelangelo Buonarroti, a young apprentice artist and sculptor who at that time was studying with Leonardo da Vinci at the conservatory. Michelangelo, Leonardo and a few others were members of what Mother called the bohemian group. I liked them.

At first, Mother tried to discourage Marie Angela from associating with artists, actors and musicians and others whom she called empty-headed. Mother said they were unpredictable as suitors and prospective husbands. She never explained any more. I thought the next time I had a few hours, I would ask Uncle Giovanni about bohemians.

Mother's feelings about performers and artists seemed to change when my brother, Vincenzo, started showing artistic abilities. The professor of music and dance at the University of Florence said Vincenzo had exceptional grace and talent. After Mother enrolled him in class, she no longer considered all bohemians bad, just different. She said we should accept people from diverse cultures based on their efforts and skills. We can learn from everyone we meet, regardless of their background.

> *We should accept people from diverse cultures based on their efforts and skills. We can learn from everyone we meet, regardless of their background.*

Before the show started, Grandfather called *Signore* Bugatti, *Signore* Mandaro, *Zio* Giovanni and the *Monsignore* off to the side for a brief discussion.

"Papa, do you want me to join you?"

"No, Giuseppe, you are too young to be concerned with these heavy matters. You relax and entertain the ladies, we will be there shortly."

With all the turmoil in the church, local politics, fear of invasion from another country and other topics of serious interest, there was much they could have been talking about. I was upset about not being invited to the meeting.

The show was wonderful. In every scene, Vincenzo was either solo on stage or in the middle of the others. He was magnificent. God gave him a special talent, and you could see he enjoyed sharing it with the audience as much as the audience enjoyed the performance. It was a blessing that Mama did not insist that he go into the fabrics business with Grandfather.

In one part of the show, Vincenzo had on a black and white silk costume with markings like a cat. His wig, makeup, and cat-like movements added to the realism of the performance. The scene opened with him being let down on stage by a rope suspended from the rafters. When on stage, he jumped and twisted like a real cat. Vincenzo said he had learned some of the special jumps from the gypsies when they camped on the outskirts of town the previous summer. He said that the gypsies had called the leaps "rushkies." Now everyone in the dance company calls them rushkies.

The summer before, when Vincenzo told me about visiting and spending time with the gypsies, he invited me to join him, saying that maybe I could learn some of their peddling techniques. He said they were really making plenty of money by mixing inexpensive oil with some scent and selling it as a cure-all for many diseases and maladies. Townspeople from Florence were evidently buying many bottles of this product. Vincenzo commented that some of them were pulling their cloak hoods over their face so that no one would recognize them. He thought he had recognized even the *Monsignore's* cloak in the crowd, but he could not see his face.

Vincenzo would say, "Pepe, these gypsies, they are some drummers and peddlers. They could make you believe anything, then sell it to you. They showed me all their secrets. They liked my dancing style, and we did a few steps together. I showed them some tap steps and they showed me leaps, twists and the rushkie split." It was obvious he enjoyed the time spent with the gypsies. He did not feel threatened by their salesmanship tricks. They gave him a bottle of their cure-all. When he tried it on a muscle strain and it did not work, he threw it away.

> ೞ
> "These gypsies, they are some drummers and peddlers. They could make you believe anything, then sell it to you."
> ೞ

After the last act, the performers received thunderous applause. I was so ecstatic over Vincenzo's performance that I spontaneously jumped to my feet and started clapping my hands and shouting, "Bravo! Bravo!" There I was, standing up in our box with everyone still sitting. More and more of the audience started to stare at me.

While some in our box may have felt embarrassed, Marie Angela took action. She tried to pull me down as she attempted to slide under the seat so no one would notice her or us, particularly Master Michelangelo.

Then a few people from the box in front of ours, occupied by the Medici family, started to stand. When *Signore* Medici, patriarch of the family, stood up it brought immediate action. Almost as if on orders, everyone in the *teatro* stood up and applauded as they shouted, "Bravo! Bravo!"

The performers, still on stage, were overwhelmed. They kept bowing and waving.

Marie Angela then stood up proudly and applauded with gusto. She shouted, "That is my brother, Vincenzo." In her hand was a special *mazzo di fiori* she had picked from our garden. She had planned to give them to Vincenzo back stage after the show, but she was so enraptured with the spontaneity of the occasion that when he looked up to wave at the family, she threw the flowers on stage. Vincenzo picked them up and threw a series of kisses to everyone in our box. No one had ever thrown flowers on the stage before that night at the *teatro* in Florence. Marie Angela was the first. It was a beautiful scene.

Vincenzo looked up again and, with flowers in hand, threw a kiss to Mama. He gave a special bow to the Medici family, patrons of the arts in Florence, builders of the *teatro* and supporters of the dance troupe.

Later, Mother mentioned that my standing up, Marie Angela's throwing flowers on stage, and Vincenzo's performance were all signs that we were passing through another stage of maturity. Mother also said my father would have been proud of all his children this night, just as she was. She commented that Father was watching us from above. I knew my father would not have missed this show. It was a wonderful occasion.

Everyone in our box talked about the outstanding performance of the dance troupe. The Medici family, including *Signore* Medici himself, came over to our box and congratulated Mama and hugged all of us. Like many Italians, he is a very warm and emotional man. Grandfather kept saying, *"Famiglia mia, famiglia mia,* my family. Vincenzo, Vincenzo, son of my son." Mama kept saying, "My babies, my babies."

CHAPTER 4

Invitations to Start My Training

The Sources of Sales Wisdom

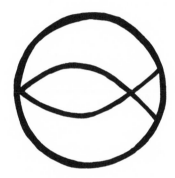

After the show, we went backstage to share our excitement with my brother. It was wonderful. Mama was proud. As she hugged Vincenzo, a tear came to her eye. "Little Vincenzo, your father would have been so proud. I know he is watching from above." We all left the theatre to go home.

As we were waiting for our carriage to be brought from the stable, *Monsignore* Mazza came over and asked if I would come over to the church to see him the next evening.

"*Monsignore,*" I said, "You know I always attend Mass with my family every Sunday. We always go to the nine o'clock service. Do you want to meet afterwards?"

"Pepe, I know you and your family are at Mass every Sunday. I would like to talk to you alone for a little while. Could you come over about four o'clock? I have a baptism tomorrow after-noon at three o'clock. The Pirellis are baptizing their seventh child, baby Rocco Nunzio Pirelli. I am not sure if that is the fifth or sixth boy. When they all get big, he will have many helpers on the farm. God bless them."

I wanted to ask the *Monsignore* what he wanted to talk about, but I knew it would be rude. He knew my grandfather and family too well for me to be inquisitive. I just said I would be at the church at four in the afternoon and bid him good night.

As I was about to get into the coach with my mother and sister I heard, "Giuseppe, Master Giuseppe Pesce, can you come here?" I turned and saw that it was *Signore* Bugatti, *Nonno's* largest cus-tomer. I went to him.

"*Si, Signor* Bugatti, *buona sera*, good evening."

"Giuseppe, your grandfather tells me you are taking a more active sales role in the House of Pesce. You are a sales appren-tice and traveling into the territory. Are you excited about this course of events? Usually salesmen do not go into the territory until they are older, at least twenty-five years old. What are you—twenty-two, twenty-three?"

"Thank you for your interest, *Signor* Bugatti. I am nineteen, and I have only been in the territory for a short period. I pray that I will do well. Although I have not sold many bolts of fabrics so far, and no pigeons have been released, I am determined to do better. Thank God my grandfather is a patient man."

"Giuseppe, you know my business. It is here in Florence. Your grandfather tells me that I am one of the biggest customers of the House of Pesce. I was one of your grandfather's first cus-tomers when he went into business over thirty years ago. My company sews all the uniforms for the province militia and pro-vides all the ceremonial robes, tunics, curtains, draperies and tapestries for the Medici family. We sew all their furniture cover-ings. Of course, you know who they are, do you not?"

"Si, *Signor* Bugatti, I know of the Medici family."

"*Bene*, I would like to help you get started as a sales appren-tice. Can you come to my place of business on Monday, if you are not on the road?"

I got the impression that he already knew I would not be in the territory on Monday—not while my wagon was in the blacksmith's shop being repaired. Just to test my grandfather's resolve to train me to be a successful sales master and to determine his commitment of support from *Signore* Bugatti, I thought I would check for a reaction with a question.

"Oh, *grazie, Signor* Bugatti. I sincerely appreciate your offer of support. However, I do not want to inconvenience you in any manner, particularly on such short notice. You must be extremely busy with more pressing matters. Maybe we can schedule a meeting at a more opportune time. Would that be acceptable?"

I guess Grandfather had clearly and convincingly expressed the depth of my depressing results from my last trip into the territory, because *Signore* Bugatti was insistent and got right to the point.

"Giuseppe, I understand that the axle broke on your wagon last Friday so you cannot go into the territory on Monday."

In an attempt not to hurt my feelings and be diplomatic, he did not ask how the axle broke, but made an approach that showed his real concern for my well being.

"Ha! It must be the Florence roads. The town council recently raised taxes again specifically for road repairs. The money was probably used to bribe an indulgence from a papal emissary. What a shame."

I did not know how much Grandfather knew or told him about how the axle broke, so I attempted a general response.

"No, *Signor* Bugatti, it was not the roads, although some are in need of repair. I was off the road riding in a meadow when the front right wheel slid into a large hole and the axle snapped. It will be fixed next week."

If Grandfather heard that I was not receptive to meeting with our largest customer, he would feel that I am not serious about my training to be a successful sales master. I took the positive approach.

"*Signor* Bugatti, I would like to visit you on Monday, although I will not be prepared to make a presentation or take any orders. As you know, Michael LaMagna is the salesman assigned to your account. Michael is the best sales master at the House of Pesce. Is he not serving you properly?"

"Ahhh! *Si*, Pepe, Michael is doing a excellent job. He is an outstanding salesman, very professional. But, Pepe, I want to see you to share some ideas on what I have noticed in the best of the salesmen who call on me to solicit my business. Maybe my observations will help you. Could you come over on Monday afternoon between two and three o'clock?"

"Si, *Signor* Bugatti, I would be pleased to visit you. Thank you very much. I hope you and *Signora* Bugatti have a restful Sunday. See you on Monday. *Ciao*."

"*Ciao*, Giuseppe."

As I headed over to the carriage, I thought about my last two conversations. Within five minutes I had talked to the *Monsignore* and *Signore* Bugatti, and both were interested in helping me to start my career as a sales apprentice. It appeared that my grandfather had already started the training program and solicited the help of some of his friends, including the clergy. It did not surprise me, because Grandfather was a very influential man, and those he associated with were always anxious to return his favors.

I felt that I was really going to enjoy the sales apprentice training program. Maybe, just maybe, it would help me to be as successful as my father. I prayed every night that I would do well. I wanted to carry on the tradition started by Grandfather and continued by my father. Oh, how I wished my father were still alive to show me the way. I knew he would have gone into the territory with me as I started my training.

> ✠
> *You go to see these gentlemen and listen to their words very closely. They possess wisdom of life and commerce that will benefit you. They are masters in their own right.*
> ✠

Mother called, "Pepe! Are you dreaming? Watch your step and get into the wagon. We are all waiting for you. What did you talk to the *Monsignore* and *Signore* Bugatti about?"

"Oh, Mama, they just wanted to talk to me about my position as a sales apprentice for the House of Pesce. I think Grandfather told them of my difficulties and they are anxious to help me."

"Giuseppe, you go to see these gentlemen and listen to their words very closely. They possess wisdom of life and commerce that will benefit you. They are masters in their own right, similar to the masters of the arts. God bless you and your grandfather."

"Mother, what does the *Monsignore* know about commerce?

He has been in a monastery and the priesthood since he was twelve years old."

"My son, the *Monsignore* has plenty of insight when it comes to commerce and success as a salesman. Is not the saving of souls and convincing others to follow the Ten Commandments a sales challenge? Of course, it is. You listen to the *Monsignore* and *Signore* Bugatti. They will help you. Along with Grandfather and *Zio* Giovanni, they will also help you become a successful sales master for the House of Pesce. Do you agree, my son?"

"*Si,* Mama, *si.* I will become a successful sales master. I will listen, ask questions, and write down the details. With their help, and by the grace of God, I will succeed."

"I know you will, I know you will. God watches over you."

> ✂
> *I will become a successful sales master. I will listen, ask questions, and write down the details. With their help and by the grace of God, I will succeed.*
> ✂

CHAPTER 5

Grandfather Introduces the Chronicles

The Importance of Recording Proven Sales Skills

That Sunday, from church, I went to talk to Grandfather. He said it was time to start listing the key characteristics that I, and all sales masters, should possess on the journey to success. He suggested that I record them on parchment paper to make it easy to refer to these essential actions and recall them as required. This way, I could review them while I traveled in the territory. He said we should call them salesmanship Chronicles. At every opportunity where I had a chance to identify a useful idea or concept for becoming an effective salesperson, I should write the key points in my Chronicles.

Once our initial training was complete, and the information

was documented with key instructions and actions required of a sales master, Grandfather planned to take it to one of his publisher friends. Printing had become much more convenient because a few years earlier a German printer named Johann Gutenberg invented a printing press using movable type. Grandfather said publishers in Florence were printing scholarly works, and copies were being distributed throughout the world. He was very proud because Florentine intellectuals were leading the world in translating and printing the classics of Greek scholars.

Grandfather knew a few publishers very well. Some of them borrowed money from him through the years. *Signore* Recordo, the publisher of *The Florence Journale*, the weekly newspaper, bought a Gutenberg press with money Papa lent him. Papa said that *Signore* Recordo would print the salesmanship Chronicles when I completed them.

> CREO
> *Information written on a page will not help our competitors unless they can implement what you write and what you do better than you.*
> CREO

Grandfather said we would distribute copies to all the sales apprentices and masters in the House of Pesce. In fact, Grandfather said he would donate copies to the public and private libraries, as well as to his business friends. Distribute the salesmanship Chronicles, my Chronicles, to others? Including competitors? I was taken by surprise.

"Papa, why do you want to share our success findings with others? Would not our competitors use this information against us?"

"Pepe, information written on a page will not help our competitors unless they can implement what you write and what you do better than you. What you record will essentially be no different than the principles for a successful life written in the classics, in the Bible, or in the works of St. Francis of Assisi. If you are confident you can apply the principles in your Chronicles in a positive, persistent, enthusiastic manner, then it makes no difference who knows. My Giuseppe, are you confident that you will seek out the knowledge and acquire the essential attitudes?"

"*Si*, Papa. It does not matter who knows what I know. I will be very successful! My belief in the House of Pesce, our fabrics and service, and myself as a sales apprentice are so great that it will overcome any temporary obstacle. My efforts will determine my success, not those of my competition."

"Giuseppe, with that statement I know you are now on your way to becoming an outstanding sales master for the House of Pesce! We will print your Chronicles and share it with anyone in the world who has an interest. Pepe, let me tell you about my first meeting with Johann Gutenberg. I had dinner with him when he was in Florence a few years ago. He gave me a Mazzarian Bible that was printed on his new press." Later, Papa told me that was the day he loaned the money to Mr. Recordo to buy a press for his Florentine newspaper.

Grandfather said that because *Signore* Gutenberg had developed his printing press, there would be many books written on a variety of subjects, conveniently copied, and widely distributed. These books, each informing or entertaining the reader, would now be available to many more people. Indeed, the printing press would really revolutionize communications. Now, many copies of a single work could be easily produced and distributed among large numbers of people.

> ✑
> *Our products and service, and myself as a sales apprentice are so great that it will overcome any temporary obstacle. My efforts will determine my success, not those of my competition.*
> ✑

"I will be the first person to prepare a manual of instructions and actions for success as a sales master," he said with pride. "It will be for the House of Pesce and others who have an interest."

Grandfather leaned back in his chair and said, "There is no doubt that many of my publishing friends would be honored to print the first sales training manual in the world for me and the House of Pesce, particularly if I remind them of the money they owe me. However, I will give Nunzio Recordo the privilege. He owes me the most."

I was excited about preparing the Chronicles, and I was learning that you can obtain much information by asking questions. "Papa, *Monsignore* Mazza says the Bible is the best instruction manual in the world for doing anything. Will our Chronicles be better than the . . . better than the . . ." I had trouble bringing out the words, "better than the Bible?"

"No, my little Giuseppe, our book will not be better than the Bible. No book can ever be better than the Bible. The Bible is the inspired word of God. Our salesmanship Chronicles will only be your words, and the understanding you get when speaking with me, Uncle Giovanni, *the Monsignore* and others who can help you grow and be successful as a sales master. The Bible is extremely helpful, if its principles are applied. It should be your guide to help you now and in the life hereafter. The contents of your Chronicles will be helpful to those aspiring to be successful sales masters. The Chronicles will be your written contribution. We can consider it your master work. Just as the beautiful paintings and statues being completed by the very talented masters presently in Florence are of value to the viewer, the Chronicles will be your contribution to the selling arts." With a smile he said, "Salespeople are artisans!"

> ೦೪୫০
> **The Chronicles will be your contribution to the selling arts. . . . Salespeople are artisans!**
> ೦೪୫০

"*Si*, Papa, being a successful sales master requires the same diligence and talent as becoming a master artist. Although I do not think that my Chronicles will be a classic, they will have the keys for success for those who apply their principles."

With a tear in his eye he said, "Pepe, I neglected to ask your father to write down all these key actions as I took him under my tutelage. It would have made it so much easier for you if this instruction had been written. I am sorry. Let us not make the same mistake again. If you write down these keys as you learn them, then we know it will be done. Do you agree, Pepe, that keeping a record of these actions will be worthwhile?"

"Of course, Grandfather. As I understand and learn the essentials for success as a sales master, I will write them down in the Chronicles." I bid Grandfather *arrivederci* and left. I was already looking ahead to writing the first document ever prepared to help me and others succeed in sales. I ran home and made the first entry of key points in my Chronicles.

Key Points in My Chronicles

- My success as a sales master will be based on what I know, my ability to apply what I know, and my attitude. I must identify my strengths and weaknesses in all areas.

- A sales master must always bounce back from temporary discouragements. I will enter each customer discussion believing that I have something of value to present.

- The sales master must visualize success before starting, just as Leonardo da Vinci did when he designed and built a new structure.

- Sales masters, like other artists, must continually practice to improve or sharpen their talents. I must never be satisfied with my present level of performance.

- I will be disciplined and continually write down key points in my Chronicles. I will use them as a guide to improve as a sales professional.

CHAPTER 6

I Go to See Monsignore Mazza

Introducing Attitudes, Skills, and Knowledge

On Sunday afternoon, I arrived at the Regina Pacis Church where *Monsignore* Ernesto Mazza is the pastor. It is a very large church built many years ago. The cornerstone read "MCDXXXVIII A.D."

I hurried in a side door, quickly dipped my hand into the holy water font, did a half genuflect towards the altar as I blessed myself and rushed to the *Monsignore's* study.

Behind the altar, *Monsignore* Mazza had his living quarters. I knocked on the entrance door and the housekeeper, *Signora* Silipigni, opened it and let me in.

"*Buon giorno*, good evening, Master Pesce. How are you today?"

29

"*Molto bene*, very well, *Signora* Silipigni, and you?"

"*Bene, grazie.*" Mrs. Silipigni had known me and my family for many years. She had been the housekeeper at the church for over twenty-five years. She even remembered my father when he was an altar boy at Regina Pacis.

As we chatted, *Monsignore* Mazza came in the entrance foyer and directed me to his study. I had been in that room many times as I tried to learn Latin so I could be an altar boy. It is a most difficult language. I have long since forgotten how to conjugate irregular Latin verbs. Someone told me in the years of the Roman Empire, the Romans would not have had much time left for conquering the world if they had to first learn Latin. I memorized my required Latin so I could become an altar boy. I had no idea what I was saying. I know the Lord forgave me.

The *Monsignore's* study was full of books. Many paintings and tapestries adorned the walls. It was well-appointed and cozy. There was a small fire in the hearth to warm the cool fall air. He motioned me to a table where he had a few quill pens. Two large candles kept the room lit.

"Giuseppe, your grandfather mentioned the frustration you are experiencing as you start your career as a sales apprentice. He has asked me to talk to you. Is that acceptable to you? Would you like me to support your grandfather in this learning process?"

"*Monsignore*, I am thankful for all the help I can get. It is welcome. Where do we start?"

"Pepe, this visit is about helping you to become all that God intended you to be, yes?"

"*Si, Monsignore.*"

"Well, Pepe, I am not knowledgeable in the specific business of fabrics and commerce. I have spent my entire life, since I was twelve, studying the Bible, reading, and learning human behavior. I feel this training and my responsibilities as a parish priest and pastor help me in understanding how to build personal relationships between individuals. This is where I can help you."

"*Monsignore*, please explain why building individual relationships is important. I am trying to sell fabrics, not collect votes as a politician."

"Pepe, building relationships helps you to sell more fabrics. You will see. Are not your grandfather and *Signore* Bugatti very good friends? Pepe, building relationships means working on your behavior. Sometimes you must adjust what you say or do. One of the most important behaviors is getting your mind focused properly before you engage in any endeavor. No matter what enterprise you are engaged in, it will only be successful if you are focused and have a strong commitment to what you are doing. Let me explain."

He positioned a piece of paper in the center of the desk and said, "Let us begin. Are you ready for the journey, Master Pesce?"

"*Si, Monsignore.* Please proceed."

Picking up a pen and dipping it into the ink from India, he drew a large triangle on the paper, then divided it off into three sections by drawing two lines parallel to the base line.

"In all of life's activities your success will be in direct relationship to how you perform in these areas. You see, this triangle is similar in shape to the pyramids of Egypt. The principles I will cover are just as long-lasting as the pyramids. They are truths— and truths are not based on time—they are enduring."

"Also, Pepe, the number three is significant. There are three focuses of our religion. We talk about and reflect on the Father, the Son and the Holy Ghost."

"*Si, Monsignore.*"

He continued, picking up the pen.

"The foundation of success is knowledge, and knowledge builds confidence. That means you must study the essential areas that make you confident." As he was speaking he wrote 'knowledge' in the bottom section of the triangle.

"Your grandfather and others who know the fabrics business, including *Signore* Bugatti, will give you the specifics of what you must learn. They can teach you about the business of selling fabric. You should listen to them. Do you agree that you must be knowledgeable about the fabric business, or any business in which you are engaged, as the basis for representing your business?"

"*Si, Monsignore.* However, I have been involved in my grandfather's business for over ten years. I started as a young boy going into the barn to tend to the horses and pigeons. I went there after the monastery school. Then I went into the warehouse to help unload the boats that brought fabrics up the Arno river from the Tyrrhenian Sea. I counted and verified incoming goods. I also kept track of each salesman's wagon inventory. Does this make me knowledgeable about the business?"

"Of course, it does, Pepe. Of course, it does. That is good, sound information. However, you must know more about the commercial selling part of the business to be a successful sales master. Suffice it to say that you must be equipped with the knowledge essential to respond to a merchant-customer's inquiry. Do you agree?"

> ০৪৪১
> *Knowledge in and of itself is not power. It is not! Knowledge is only potential power. Only when you can communicate effectively what you know will you benefit.*
> ০৪৪১

"*Si, Monsignore.* When you know something you become confident. You are powerful."

"Giuseppe, knowledge in and of itself is not power. It is not! Knowledge is only potential power. Only when you can communicate effectively what you know will you benefit. As a peddler salesman you must communicate so that your customer is persuaded. But be careful, my Pepe, the power of persuasion is very strong. It can be used for good or it can be used for evil. Let me give you an example. Do you remember last summer when a small caravan of gypsies passed through town and set up camp on the plains just north of the city?"

"*Si, Monsignore.*"

"I went there and enjoyed watching the dancing and music, Giuseppe. It was a pleasant evening. When the performance was over, a man started selling a special elixir; he called it 'Godsend.' He said he had developed it as a cure for many maladies, including a pain in the shoulder which I had been experiencing at the time. He was a real drummer. In fact, someone in the crowd who saw me rub my shoulder said that he had bought a bottle, and it had cured him overnight. Others proclaimed that it had cured them from sprained knees, twisted ankles, even hair loss. Within a few minutes, the hawker had the crowd so whipped up with excitement that he sold over fifty bottles of his 'Godsend' elixir, his total supply."

I interjected, "Oh, *Monsignore*, he was a very professional sales master to sell his total supply."

"No, Giuseppe, just the opposite, he was a charlatan."

"Why, *Monsignore?*"

"Because he told a falsehood about his product. Pepe, the elixir he sold was ineffective. He intentionally sold a product that did not do what he said—he misrepresented. He sold false dreams and hopes, a cure for pain. Our local chemist says it is merely extra virgin olive oil with a few drops of perfume for a pleasant smell and a portion of black fig juice to give it an unusual mystic pale purple color. He says it has no qualities known to be a cure for the maladies mentioned.

Giuseppe, I mention this incident because many people will listen to a persuasive speaker and sales master. Again, this is a power that can be used for good or for evil. As you proceed on your journey to become a successful sales apprentice for the House of Pesce, make sure you use this persuasive power for good. Your grandfather and your father, may he rest in peace, would want it that way."

> ৫৪৩৪
> *Many people will listen to a persuasive speaker and sales master. . . this is a power that can be used for good or evil. . . . make sure you use this persuasive power for good.*
> ৫৪৩৪

"I will, *Monsignore,* I will."

"Pepe, honestly is the only way your Grandfather would want you to represent the products of the House of Pesce. Never misrepresent. By being truthful, you build long-term relations with people. Do you agree?"

"*Si, Monsignore.*"

"Knowledge is also important in developing trusting relationships. You must know what products your customers use, what business they are in, their likes and dislikes. This is important in building trusting relationships. Do you understand?"

"*Si, Monsignore.*" I was not really sure I understood everything, but I could think about it. I still had a couple of questions to ask before I left.

"*Monsignore,* what are the other two parts of the triangle on top of the knowledge base?"

Picking up the pen, he wrote in two words. First, *Skills* in the middle segment and then *Attitude* on the top.

"Pepe, the middle segment represents all the skills you must acquire to communicate the knowledge that you have. These will be the sales skills you learn from your grandfather, *Signore* Bugatti, your uncle, and others, and the relationship building we just spoke of. More important than the skills and knowledge are all the attitudes you must have to succeed. My son, the attitudes that you have or develop will be the driving force that ultimately determine the level of success you achieve in sales and in life. You must always be self-motivated and want to succeed in whatever you do! I am sure your grandfather and others whom you talk with will help you in these key areas. We will talk again on attitudes.

> *"Ask and you shall receive, seek and you shall find, knock and it shall be opened unto you."* Remember this verse as you progress in your training.

"Look at the first letters in the words *attitude, skills* and *knowledge*. They spell the word *ask*. You have got to ask for business. You have got to ask others how they can help you grow in your profession. St. Matthew says 'Ask and you shall receive, seek and you shall find, knock and it shall be opened unto you.' (Matthew 7:7) Remember this verse as you progress in your training.

Pepe, now the hour is getting late. Take this parchment with the triangle and show it to your grandfather. Ask him to proceed by identifying the specific areas in which you must be proficient. Is that agreeable to you?"

"*Si, Monsignore*, I will do it, and I appreciate the time we spent together tonight. *Grazie, molto grazie.*"

"It is my pleasure, my son, *buona notte*, good night. Go, peace be with you. Please come by again Wednesday evening about eight. I have a friend, another man of God, I want you to meet."

I took many notes that day. The next day I would spend reviewing them with Grandfather before I visited *Signore* Bugatti in the afternoon. There would be time to learn.

Key Points in My Chronicles

———— ∞ ————

⊖ Success as a sales master will be based on what I know about my products and services, my customers, and my competitors. The more I know, the better prepared I will be.

⊖ Knowledge is not power unless I can clearly communicate what I know to others. I must be a master communicator through my speaking, listening, and writing.

⊖ Once I am comfortable with my knowledge and my communication skills, then I must strive to meet as many customers as possible. The more I meet, the better my opportunities for a sale.

⊖ For long-term success, I must have many key attitudes, particularly self-motivation, persistence, and enthusiasm.

⊖ Honesty is critical and basic. Customers must trust me and what I say.

⊖ In order to get business and to get help in my sales profession, I must learn to ask for what I want.

CHAPTER 7

A Visit to Our Biggest Customer

Learning the Source and Value of Enthusiasm

On Monday afternoon, I had an opportunity to visit *Signore* Gregorio Bugatti at his place of business, *Creations by Bugatti*. *Signore* Bugatti and his team of designers, pattern-makers and seamstresses are in the business of creating and selling garments, draperies, furniture coverings, church vestments, and tapestries to some of the most prominent families in Florence and many towns around. He has customers as far away as Roma, Napoli, and Venezia. Their famous customers include the Borges, the Tosi and the Medici families.

Before I left to see *Signore* Bugatti, Grandfather gave me a bolt of his newest silk fabric as a present for *Signora* Bugatti.

He said there was enough material to make a beautiful dress for the *Signora* and her granddaughter, Concetta Bartolommeo. The Bugattis had been the guardians of Concetta since her parents died of the Black Plague about the same time as my father. Concetta's mother was the Bugattis' oldest daughter. My grandfather and *Signore* Bugatti had been trying to make a "match" of Concetta and me for the past two years. I had not resisted. She is a beautiful young woman and we enjoy being together. A short while back, we went to see one of Vincenzo's rehearsals and had a wonderful picnic together. Of course, Marie Angela and one of Concetta's aunts were with us as chaperones. I hoped that maybe after my discussion with *Signore* Bugatti, I could spend a few minutes talking with Concetta, even if it was in the presence of *Signora* Bugatti or another chaperone.

Signora Bugatti designed and made my mother's wedding gown. Mother keeps it in her wardrobe. It still looks beautiful. Marie Angela tried it on one day when Mother was out. Vincenzo and I teased her about her meetings with young Michelangelo Buonarroti. Mother had been trying to cool off that budding relationship, and she would have been very upset if she had seen Marie Angela in the dress.

Creations by Bugatti had the largest number of sewing operators in the city of Florence. *Signore* Bugatti had a sewing room in his place of business where ninety-seven women worked at large wooden tables. A much greater number of seamstresses worked in their homes. They all worked on what *Signore* Bugatti called "piece work."

Signore Bugatti explained, "It makes it easy to keep accounts of each person's productivity, and I do not have to concern myself with the women's other obligations at home. By counting finished pieces, the seamstresses decide how much they want to earn. They decide how much time they want to spend working versus the time they spend in other activities. The in-home seamstresses like this method, particularly if they have small children, elderly parents, or other obligations. Every week I send a wagon to the home of each seamstress. We pick up the finished goods and drop off new, precut materials for the following week."

Signore Bugatti felt that in time more people would be working out of the home. It allows the seamstresses to spend more time sewing and less time dressing, traveling, and preparing meals to eat at the shop. This was very forward thinking by *Signore* Bugatti.

"Each year more and more people decide to work from their house," he said, "and I have been very happy with the results so far."

I wanted to know more about this man and his magnificent business.

"*Signor* Bugatti, it is very kind of you to offer to see me. I am thankful for your concern and your time. I want to become the most successful sales master ever in the history of the House of Pesce. You have known my grandfather many years?"

"*Si*, Giuseppe, I have known your grandfather for over thirty years. It is my pleasure to help you on your journey. I also helped your father, probably fifteen years ago."

After thanking him again for taking the time to help, I told him about my regular entries in the salesmanship Chronicles I was preparing.

"*Signor* Bugatti, what do you feel is required to be a successful sales master?"

> ⊂℈⊃
> *Nothing great can be accomplished without a certain fervor, intensity, and excitement that are joined with faith, courage and hopefulness. This is what makes enthusiasm.*
> ⊂℈⊃

"My Giuseppe, the one characteristic you must place in your Chronicles as absolutely essential for success as a sales apprentice is enthusiasm. Enthusiasm, my Pepe, is derived from two Greek words, *en* and *theos*, meaning 'in God' or 'a God within.' It is a strong zeal that you exhibit. It is a passion for what you are doing."

I could see that *Signore* Bugatti really wanted to spend a fair amount of time on this subject, so I moved my chair closer and opened my Chronicles so that I could take notes. He continued.

"Enthusiasm is an earnest and commendable devotion or an eager interest. Pepe, against the hindrances that a sales master faces, nothing great can be accomplished without a certain fervor, intensity and excitement that are joined with faith, courage and hopefulness. This is what makes enthusiasm."

I recognized that I wanted to get this enthusiasm.

"*Signor* Bugatti, what must I do to get this enthusiasm? If it is that important, please tell me what is the secret?"

"Giuseppe," he replied smiling, "while it is essential to have enthusiasm, you do not have to study or do much reading to get it! Enthusiasm comes from inside your heart, not from your head. My Giuseppe, you become and you act enthusiastically when what you talk about excites you. This strong conviction is heard in your voice, it is seen in the sparkle in your eyes, and it is understood because you are believable. The fervor and zeal is expressed in your total persona and those you associate with, particularly your merchant customers. We might say, without stretching the truth, that enthusiasm means being full of God. Some say that every great and commanding movement in the annals of the world is the triumph of enthusiasm. Giuseppe, your enthusiasm will fight apathy."

> ☙
> *While it is essential to have enthusiasm, you do not have to study or do much reading to get it! Enthusiasm comes from inside your heart, not from your head.*
> ❧

"Fight apathy? *Signor* Bugatti, please explain."

"The person that takes an apathetic approach says, 'Things are fine as they are, why upset the apple cart? Let us proceed as before with the tried and true and traditional. We are satisfied with the status quo. The old ways are still valid and effective.' This approach does not leave any room for moving ahead and advancing your cause. Giuseppe, neither your grandfather nor I would have ever built our businesses to their present size if we were apathetic." He took a sip from a glass of water and continued.

"Pepe, apathy can only be overcome by enthusiasm, but you have to understand enthusiasm. In the past, the word connoted fanaticism, frenzy, obsession. Now it is reserved for a sincere, earnest, active interest in our devotion to a person, idea, or cause—a devotion that is joyfully and willingly manifested. In this sense of the word, one cannot be enthusiastic about anything bad. One might be fanatical or obsessed, but not enthusiastic. Enthusiasm is reasonable. You can be enthusiastic without losing control of your emotions and resorting to frantic actions that discredit you and your cause. My son, enthusiasm is a priceless quality. We all are born with the seeds of enthusiasm, and those seeds continue to grow. Children are packed full of enthusiasm, wonder, excitement, sheer joyfulness. Unfortunately, as they get older some lose their excitement, their enthusiasm. The essence of genius is to carry the spirit of our childhood into old age, to keep the child's enthusiasm as we grow up. If we have lost it, it can be recovered, and it is worth recovering at any cost."

Signore Bugatti enjoyed discussing enthusiasm. His voice rang with emotion as he leaned forward in his large chair. His face was bright and colorful, like that of a child's, as he spoke of enthusiasm and excitement. He was extremely excited about this discussion, so I encouraged him to continue. "*Signor* Bugatti, how can I maintain the high levels of enthusiasm necessary to become a sales master?"

"Enthusiasm focuses on the positive," he answered, "instead of harping forever on the negative. Enthusiasm can criticize, but it will do so constructively, not destructively. Enthusiasm builds on the good points. It would rather rejoice that thorn bushes have roses than complain that they have thorns."

> ⊗
> *When a man dies, if he can pass enthusiasm along to his children, he has left them an estate of incalculable value.*
> ⊗

"*Signor* Bugatti, how do you know if you, or I, or others have this enthusiasm?"

"Giuseppe, when we develop enthusiasm, we discover that life has much more zest in it. Indeed, with enthusiasm life can become a series of joyful and exhilarating experiences. Where the eye is sparkling and the step sprightly, look for enthusiasm and you will find it doing its mighty work. Those who are fully alive have attractive personalities. They are nice to be with, fun to have around. Just to see them provides an emotional treat. It brightens your day and lightens your load. When enthusiasm is kindled, wonderful new things can happen."

At that time, one of his assistants came into the office with a question about the order for the Cardinal's Easter festivities. *Signore* Bugatti answered the question as he turned to me and said, "If you have enthusiasm, you will be successful. Giuseppe, when a man dies, if he can pass enthusiasm along to his children, he has left them an estate of incalculable value. Since work is a part of our everyday life, it is a very wise idea to work with enthusiasm. Things go so much better with enthusiasm. Challenges are easier to face, obstacles are more easily overcome. Enthusiasm will help you overcome the temporary setbacks you experience when those you call on may object or look unfavorably on your offering."

From that minute on, I made a strong commitment to always be enthusiastic. I stood up to leave, thanked him and gave him a big hug. There was much to enter in my Chronicles.

> ᣩᣠ
> *Things go so much better with enthusiasm. Challenges are easier to face, obstacles are more easily overcome.*
> ᣩᣠ

Key Points in My Chronicles

- ⊝ I will approach each customer with positive anticipation. I will enter believing that I will leave with an order now or bring myself closer to one in the near future.

- ⊝ My positive thinking builds self-motivation. It is a real driving force for success as a sales master. I will pursue the sales challenge with a passion that will keep me enthusiastic.

- ⊝ I firmly believe that what I take to market provides the best value to my customer—value that can be seen in both my products and my service.

- ⊝ I will refer to other satisfied customers when talking to a new prospect. Their testimonies will help show that I have products and services of value.

- ⊝ My enthusiasm will overcome any apathy that attempts to creep into my approach. Customers will want to talk to me because I am enthusiastic about my offering.

- ⊝ I will be enthusiastic about life in general and let it grow in my relationships with all people.

CHAPTER 8

Training in Florence

What it Takes to be
a Sales Professional

Grandfather saw my frustration when I asked, "Papa, it seems that there is so much I do not know about being a successful sales apprentice. Will I ever know everything? Will I ever be a success selling for the House of Pesce?"

"Pepe, my Pepe, being a successful sales master is a profession; you can never know everything about your profession. You will do fine, Pepe, and you will grow as your confidence builds and you gain experience. It will reflect on your successes."

"I pray that you are correct, Grandfather, but sometimes I have no patience. I want to be successful now; I want to fill my father's void. I want to sell more now!"

A tear filled Grandfather's eye. It seemed every time my father was mentioned, Grandfather started to recollect and become emotional, particularly at this time of the year because it was approaching Father's birthday. Grandfather composed himself and continued, "I know you are impatient, and that is a healthy sign. It means you are striving for something better. That is good. That is very good. All professionals strive for something better; all professionals strive for improvement."

"Papa, even now in this brief meeting we have discussed many things that I am uncertain about. I know they are important, but I am not sure how these ideas fit into my Chronicles. How can I include ideas in my Chronicles and refer to them while I travel if I am unclear now?"

"You are right, Pepe. We have talked of many things. Where would you like to start?"

"Papa, you spoke of professionalism, confidence, and impatience."

"*Bene*, Pepe. We will begin with confidence. You will become confident as a sales apprentice when you have a good feeling backed up with sound knowledge about the fabrics we manufacture, the businesses of our merchant customers, what they like and dislike, and, of course, what it takes to make them more successful in their business."

"Successful in *their* business, Grandfather?"

"Of course, Giuseppe, we want all our customers to be extremely successful. As they grow using our fabrics, we will grow also.

"Giuseppe, confidence does not mean one should be a braggadocio. It means you have a quiet feeling of self-assurance that you know what you are doing. Confidence will come to you. You can rest assured that in representing the House of Pesce, you are representing the best. As you become more successful, your confidence will grow. As your confidence grows, you will also become more successful."

A smile appeared on his face. He wanted me, as the newest sales apprentice of the House of Pesce, to be proud and confident. I was beginning to feel it.

"Grandfather, you mentioned about being a professional—is selling a profession? I thought that those who went to school for long periods were professionals. Like *Zio* Giovanni, who went to the university and studied law to become an *avvocato*, or *Monsignore* Mazza, who studied for years for the priesthood, or

Professore Barone, the physician. Are they not professionals? Papa, are we professionals like them?"

"Giuseppe, a person does not automatically become a professional merely by going to a university for a long period and completing a program. Professional status is an earned position based on performance, not merely on one's education."

"You see, there is a misunderstanding about what constitutes a professional. Because many people like to react to complex situations with overly simple responses, it is easy to say all vocations, all clergy, all *avvocatos*, and all physicians are professionals, and everyone else is not. That is a mistake you would not want to make."

"But, Grandfather, sales apprentices are typically not held in as high a regard as the others. I remember when I was in the monastery school, I told my classmates I wanted to be a sales master like my father and grandfather, and they laughed. They said salespeople are liars who frequently cheat the people they convince to buy their wares. I stopped telling my classmates about my aspirations and simply said I would be a 'merchandising representative' for the House of Pesce. This name change created a lot more respect from my classmates."

> ෴
> *Professional status is an earned position based on performance, not merely on one's education.*
> ෴

"Pepe, you will be a sales professional regardless of the name if you continually strive to improve your abilities to serve those with whom you deal and are sincerely interested in doing what is best for them. There are numerous stories about those that practice the law or medicine, or are in the priesthood, who have not performed in a professional manner. You can ask *Zio* Giovanni or *Monsignore* Mazza or *Professore* Barone. They are professionals, but they know of others in their ranks who are not. Sometimes, Pepe, because of a few, unscrupulous individuals in sales, outsiders are fast to criticize the entire group. Selling is a noble profession, my grandson."

"A noble profession, Grandfather?"

"*Si*, the ideas that we turn into products and services help the people who buy from us improve their way of life. Let me explain. Many say that the wheel was the most significant discovery to date. I am not sure if it is. Some believe Johann Gutenberg's press may be. We will see. Pepe, if thousands of years ago when the wheel was developed as an ideal way of moving objects, if the person who discovered this simple device said, 'I will keep it for myself,' would we have progressed this far? No, the inventor was very anxious to share this new idea. He quickly had to supply wheels to others. Pepe, although you may have difficulty seeing it now, do you realize that a strong conviction in the wheel product gave the inventor the confidence to want to tell others? He was indeed a sales master."

"Grandfather, is the discoverer of the wheel recorded?"

"No, Giuseppe, the details are sketchy as to the name of any individual discoverer, but there are paintings in caves indicating that it was many thousands of years ago. It was probably discovered in Egypt. Many inventions are typically developed out of necessity. Undoubtedly, in Egypt it was necessary because they had to move very large stones to put them in place for the pyramids. Pepe, if it was not for the wheel, Michelangelo Buonarroti would never have been able to get that huge piece of marble he is working on from the quarry to his studio. Remember, I told you about my meeting with Johann Gutenberg?"

> *If you continue to look for ways to improve your knowledge and skills, plus show a willingness to serve your customers, you are a sales professional. Remember, you must never stop learning. School is never out for the professional.*

"Yes, Papa, you told me that after he demonstrated his invention, this printing press, you and *Signore* Recordo of *The Florence Journal* decided to buy it."

"Yes, Giuseppe, *Signore* Gutenberg was so excited and enthusiastic about his invention that the enthusiasm was contagious, and we realized the long-term advantages of having a machine that can print many copies. That is the enthusiasm a professional sales master must have. Giuseppe, if you continue to look for ways to improve your knowledge and skills, plus show a willingness to serve your customers, you are a sales professional. Remember, you must never stop learning. School is never out for the professional."

"Grandfather, it seems that it is very difficult to be a successful sales master! Will I ever learn everything I need to learn?"

"Of course, you will, my son. If you learn what we teach you and apply those skills, you will do well. Remember to keep your records up-to-date. Each day enter the key traits you learned into your Chronicles. Add your comments on how you apply your skills as you travel the territory. Now, for today, we discussed the importance of confidence and professionalism. We also touched on having enthusiasm."

"*Si*, Papa, but you also spoke of impatience."

"Impatience *and* patience, my Pepe. Impatience is your motivator. You must always want to know more, learn more, sell more. Now! Patience means that you will persevere and be steadfast. You will continue to try to serve your customers, even when they are buying another's fabrics. You will take all the right actions and not waver. By doing this, you will be successful. When your patience grows thin and impatience seems to be taking over, remember this short prayer: 'God grant me the courage to change the things I can, the serenity to accept those I cannot, and the wisdom to know the difference.'"

> ☙❧
> *God grant me the courage to change the things I can, the serenity to accept those I cannot, and the wisdom to know the difference.*
> ☙❧

I could see my grandfather was getting tired.

"Papa, we spent a very wonderful time learning today, and I love you for it. The hour is late. Are there any additional comments about patience you want to make before I go home for the night?"

"Yes, Pepe, there are other scriptures in the Bible that relate to patience as well. Please ask the *Monsignore* the exact locations where they can be found, so that you can enter the passages in your Chronicles. Your Chronicles, when completed, will be an ideal resource as you continue your journey to become a professional sales master."

The next day I would visit Uncle Giovanni in the afternoon and the *Monsignore* at night. When I made my entry in the Chronicles that night, I wrote key points of my discussion with Grandfather, including the scripture from the Bible which he spoke of. It was in Ecclesiastics 3:1–2. I will read it every day because it is an inspiring message.

> *To everything there is a season,*
> *A time for every purpose under heaven:*
> *A time to be born,*
> *And a time to die:*
> *A time to plant,*
> *And a time to pluck what is planted.*

Key Points in My Chronicles

⊖ For continuous development, I will list the areas that need improvement, then commit myself to a program that gets me to the desired level. My improvements must be measurable and completed by a certain date.

⊖ I must never be satisfied with anything less than my best. When I am not performing my best, I must improve.

⊖ Confidence comes from knowledge; therefore, I must never stop learning.

⊖ Both impatience and patience are important to the successful sales master. I must be *impatient* with my progress, particularly if I do not have a self-improvement program in place. I must be *patient* if I am involved in a self-improvement program and it is taking longer than expected to show results.

⊖ Everything worthwhile requires salesmanship, so I will have pride in my profession.

CHAPTER 9

𝒜 Visit Uncle Giovanni

Suggestions for Persuading Customers

A visit to Uncle Giovanni and Aunt Catherine was always a pleasure. I think they are my favorite *zio* and *zia*. This may be because they did not have any children, and I am the oldest son of Vincenzo, Uncle Giovanni's only brother.

Zio Giovanni made a vow to my father when Father was on his death bed. Uncle Giovanni told Father that he would look after the family. He took his promise to my father very seriously.

Their home was close to ours, about a half kilometer away. Uncle Giovanni is a really unique individual, and I could spend hours listening to him. He is a brilliant attorney, an *avvocato*. He is also an amateur inventor, a woodworking craftsman, an accomplished gardener, and a wine and spirits maker.

When approaching his home, one immediately noticed his brightly painted sign in the shape of a fish hanging from a post. It was about a half-meter long and twenty centimeters wide, and read *Casa Pesce, Giovanni Pesce, Avvocato, Consigliere,* in large white letters.

Zio Giovanni was employed by Grandfather for a few years as a sales apprentice during summer sabbaticals from the University of Roma Law Conservatory. Grandfather said he was a terrific sales apprentice, very persuasive, with patience and persistence. He never gave up. One of Uncle's most frequently used words when talking to a customer was *perche*, why?

Vincenzo, my father, the oldest son, was destined to be Grandfather's successor. Father died last year. His untimely death changed all of Grandfather's plans to reduce his activities and take it easier. Now, Grandfather is working as hard as ever and we are all worried about his health, although his doctors say he is in excellent condition.

Grandfather believes his diet is one that, in time, all followers of good health will use. He assures anyone he talks with that his eating habits work because they do not make him sluggish or overweight. Grandfather says that his daily meals include plenty of fruit and vegetables, many legumes, fresh garlic and pasta. He also eats plenty of raw and cooked garlic with his salads and sauces, plus a glass or two of wine with his meals. Papa eats very little red meat, mostly fish and chicken. Plus he walks every day during the business day and also during the evenings in his orchard. It must work because there are many, much younger employees in the House of Pesce who cannot keep up with him.

It will take time for Grandfather to get over my father's death. He and Grandmother both took the loss very hard. We all did. Grandmother told my mother that many nights Grandfather would fall asleep in his favorite chair with his rosary beads in his hand. He could be heard crying softly, "*Perche, Gesu Cristo? Perche, Gesu Cristo?* Why?"

Why God would take a devoted family man, leaving a wife and three children is still a mystery to me. In my Bible I read, "All things work together for good to those that believe." I do not know what good has come from my father's early death, but I do know that when I meet my God, after I praise him, the first question I am going to ask is: "Lord, why did you take my father at such a young age, there was so much we never had an opportunity to talk about. What good came from his swift, untimely death? Please tell me why."

Although Grandfather was initially disappointed that his only other son, Uncle Giovanni, did not go into the family business, Grandfather never stopped encouraging my uncle to be the best he could be in whatever profession he chose. Grandpa wanted Uncle Giovanni to be the best *avvocato* in the Republic of Florence, maybe the best in all of Italy.

On that visit I had a very specific purpose. I wanted to learn from Uncle about the scales of justice that are the symbol for the legal profession. Grandfather said, "When you go over to visit *Zio* and *Zia*, have *Zio* Giovanni explain to you how the scale can help you visualize and understand some key points about success as a sales apprentice."

On the mantle over the fireplace in *Zio* and *Zia's* home was a brass statue of the blindfolded Goddess of Justice. She was holding a scale in one hand and a sword in the other.

> ০৪৪০
> *He is undoubtedly going to say 'no' to your initial approach. You must expect that. Do not take that as a personal affront. Do not be offended.*
> ০৪৪০

I asked, "Uncle Giovanni, why is she blindfolded?"

"Giuseppe, the blindfold on the goddess means that the decision reached by the parties involved should be made without prejudice. It should be based only on the evidence that is placed on each side of the scale and on which way the balance tips. Pepe, while the scales are symbolic for the legal system, they also provide a very appropriate representation for you, a young sales apprentice. Let me explain."

With Uncle Giovanni, you never had to ask for an explanation, he always proceeded without invitation.

"Pepe, let us assume that you are taking your fabrics in to a storekeeper who is already buying fabrics from someone else. He is undoubtedly going to say 'no' to your initial approach. You must expect that. Do not take that as a personal affront. Do not be offended."

"*Zio*, with repeated 'No's,' I get very withdrawn. I want to take my sample fabrics and leave immediately."

"Pepe, when the storekeeper says 'no' that is the exact time to try again. Show that you are a real Pesce. You do not give up, but like a strong, determined fish show that you can swim upstream, against the flow." That brought a smile to my face.

"What the storekeeper is really saying with his 'no' is that he does not need your products or services. He is satisfied with his present suppliers. It is not necessary for him to talk to you, another salesperson. What he means is 'why should I listen to you?'

> ᘒᘒ
> *Visualize that the scales of balance are now tipped totally to one side, all in favor of the competing salesperson. You have to get the scales balanced before there may be any interest in listening further.*
> ᘒᘒ

Visualize that the scales of balance are now tipped totally to one side, all in favor of the competing salesperson. You have to get the scales balanced before there may be any interest in listening further. Before a storekeeper will buy, you must get the scales tipped in your favor." Uncle Giovanni paused, then asked, "Pepe, do you follow this approach?"

"I am not certain, Uncle. What do I say when the storekeeper says 'no' to my approach? How do I start to tip the scales in my favor?"

"Well, Pepe, it has been a few years since I called on merchants for the House of Pesce, but let us try what *avvocatos* call a mock trial. That is, we will go through a typical meeting you may have with a customer. Pepe, you imagine that you are coming into my shop. You see by the sign that I make tapestries, draperies and dresses for ladies in the court. You feel that I would be interested in purchasing the beautiful line of fabrics made by the House of Pesce. Pepe, like a strong determined fish, start swimming upstream. What do you do, and say, as you greet the customer?"

I cleared my throat, straightened my tunic and, extending my right hand, started my approach, "*Buon giorno*. My name is Giuseppe Pesce, fabrics salesman for the House of Pesce in Florence. Can I interest you in my wares?"

Uncle Giovanni stopped me right there, with my hand still extended.

"Pepe, watch out for local traditions. Many people in the northern republics are not accustomed to that new handshaking concept. The practice was started in Rome years ago for security reasons, not as a sign of hospitality or cordiality."

"Back then, Pepe, when strangers first met each other on the road, they extended their right hands to show that neither party was carrying a knife or ax to use as a weapon and do harm. Then they held the other person's right hand and shook it a few times so that if there were a knife up a sleeve, it would fall out. Pepe, while the handshake is a good approach in Rome, Orvieto, or Assisi, be wary when you travel in the northern republics. The people in Bologna, Genoa, or Modena may not be familiar with that custom and may feel uncomfortable, particularly merchants farther north in Milan, Lodi, or Como. They surely will feel uncomfortable with this Roman handshake." He stretched, took a deep breath and continued.

"Pepe, I do not want to make a major point about this handshake. I merely want you to be aware that there are differences in the traditions, business experiences, and education of each person you meet. You must be aware of these differences. Remember, before any merchant has an interest in the House of Pesce or your fabrics, they have to trust you and believe you. Once you have that, then you can start talking specifics about your wares.

Remember, before any merchant has an interest in the House of Pesce or your fabrics, they have to trust you and believe you. Once you have that, then you can start talking specifics about your wares.

"One more point, Pepe. You should always be considerate of your time and the customer's time. You may want to use an hourglass as you practice your presentations."

As I said before, Uncle Giovanni never left a story only partially told. He always gave much more background information and details than one would expect or even be interested in. Now was no exception. He proceeded to tell me how an hourglass was made, and how the two chambers that hold the sand are connected by a narrow neck with a very precise opening. Just when I thought he was finished, he continued.

"The sand must also be of critical dimension or the hourglass will not work. If the sand is too small, it will flow through the opening very quickly. If it is too large it will block the opening, and it will not flow at all." With a smile he said, "If the hole between the chambers is too big the sand will flow very rapidly, then it will only be a half-hour glass. Or a twenty-minute glass. If the hole is too small, no sand will flow, and it will be a no hour glass. Ha!" *Zio* Giovanni frequently laughed at comments that he thought humorous. Sometimes he would be the only one laughing.

"The point is, Pepe, you must be aware of the amount of time that you spend with your customers. Your time is valuable, and so is theirs. Use time efficiently."

With that I thought surely the hour glass story was over. It was not. I should have known.

"Ischia. The Isle of Ischia, off the coast of Naples. That is where the sand for hour glasses comes from! Ischia is the only place in the discovered world where that precise sand can be found. The sand forms dunes on the northeastern coast of the island. In that one location there is the proper flow of the tides, the meeting of the colder waters from the Mediterranean Sea with the warmer waters from the Tyrrehenian Sea. Until a few years ago, the sand was being taken without any regard for conserving the shore line and natural resources." Having an interest in conservation and our natural resources, I was starting to get interested in the sand from the Isle of Ischica.

"Thankfully, the governor of the island appointed an overseer to keep watch over the sand removal. It is monitored so that it is not removed any faster than it is washed ashore by the tides and mother nature. Before there was an overseer of the sand dunes, unconcerned hourglass makers—pirates from Naples and Amalfi—would row over in their boats, filling so many barrels of sand that the boats would be heavily laden. Because of slightly rough seas, many of the pirates would be lost, and the sand returned to the sea." He added that it seemed like a high price to pay for not observing conservation.

I thought another "Oh!" and a "My Goodness!" would get him to conclude the story so that we could get back to my lesson on salesmanship. It did not. He is persistent and knowledgeable. No wonder he is one of the most sought after *consiglieres* in all of Florence. He never gives up. He is stubborn. Uncle Giovanni continued:

"The Island of Ischica, that is where your great-grandfather Giuseppe was born. He was a dock builder. He and your great-grandmother lived there all their lives. I remember when I was a small boy, your grandfather would take your father and me to visit him and Grandma Pierina. They had a wonderful home with extensive orchards of grape vines and oranges, figs, and lime trees. His olive grove was one of the best on the island. He made wine and olive oil for all his neighbors, *paesanos,* and family. When a storm destroyed the property and tore up the beautiful orchard, he and great-grandma moved to Florence and lived with *Nonno* Giuseppe and *Nonna* Carolina."

"*Zio* Giovanni, that is an interesting story, but now the hour is late. Perhaps we can continue this lesson on the scales of justice another time?"

"*Si,* Pepe. I have gone and spoken of interesting matters, but not much for a future sales master like you to use. We will continue another day. *Ciao.*"

As I left, I thought of the other visits I would make that week: one to see *Signore* Mandaro and one to see grandfather again. I was really beginning to look forward to all of these visits.

Key Points in My Chronicles

- ⊖ The scale is a convenient way for me to weigh the products and services I provide against the prices I ask.

- ⊖ I will be aware of the differences in cultures and norms and respect other traditions. I will not pre-judge a customer before getting to know the person. I will enter every discussion with a positive, open frame of mind.

- ⊖ I will be concerned with where and how I spend my time. Time is an extremely valuable resource. I will continually ask myself, "Am I receiving an equitable return for the time I invest?"

- ⊖ The sales profession requires that I have plenty of energy. I will take care of my health, watch my diet, and get enough rest.

- ⊖ I will respect my customers and be considerate of the time we spend together.

CHAPTER 10

A Visit to Mandaro's Dairy

Getting Customers Involved in Your Presentation

It was Wednesday morning when I visited Mandaro's Dairy and Cheese Company. *Signore* Mandaro said this was a slow time of the week, and we would have plenty of time to talk. Grandfather has been a long-time friend of his family, and he made sure I took over a large basket of freshly picked fruit from his orchard. Grandfather wanted to share with his *paesanos*. In addition to figs, apples, oranges, limes, and lemons, I also brought a blown crystal decanter bottle of his finest virgin olive oil and a jar of my mother's freshly made marinara sauce. Grandfather enjoyed making light of the fact that he was a few days older than *Signore* Mandaro, frequently saying he should listen to "his elders." They were *paesanos* from the Isle of Ischia. Ancestors of the Mandaro family and the Pesce family had fled during a storm that destroyed their homes. They settled side by side on the outskirts of Florence. Grandfather went into the fabrics business, and *Signore* Mandaro went into the dairy and cheese making business. That was over thirty years ago. Frequently, they go back in time and talk about the difficult times they experienced when they both started out.

> ஐௐ
> *Building a business must be based on providing outstanding products and service. Both are essential.*
> ஐௐ

There was never a fence between our properties until *Signore* Mandaro's goats and milk cow herds became so large that he thought it best to have his three sons build a low, stone wall between our properties to control the herds. I think *Signore* Mandaro decided it was time to build the wall the day he saw Vincenzo and me pulling the tail of one of his prize cows when it came on our property. His three sons, Francesco, Pietro, and Nicholas, took a few weeks to build the wall. It was about a half meter high and a meter wide. I am sure the wall would have gone up faster if they had not needed to chase Vincenzo, Marie Angela, and me as we watched and gave directions. Marie Angela and I went to the same monastery school as Nicholas' daughters—Elizabeth, Jean, and Joan. We were not related, but we were family.

Signore Mandaro was overjoyed when he saw me. He was taken aback by the gifts. With a little tear in his eye, he said it was not necessary that I bring gifts, and that it was a pleasure to see me. As we hugged, he told me to thank my grandparents and my mother. *Signore* Mandaro agreed to share his experiences on how he built his business.

"Pepe," he began, "building a business must be based on providing outstanding products and service. Both are essential areas you must understand as you seek to expand your knowledge and skills in your quest to become an outstanding sales master."

Mandaro's Dairy and Cheese Company operation was very impressive. It covered many acres. The herd of dairy cows and goats numbered over one thousand head. Besides his three sons, *Signore* Mandaro had help in running the farm from many others. The operation was one of the largest employers in the area. They provided employment for many teenagers who had lost their parents during the Black Plague. Not only did the Mandaros provide employment, they also had a boarding facility on the property that gave comfortable lodging for the youngsters. *Signore* Mandaro, working with the church orphanage, received the children when they were twelve years old. They all attended the local monastery school. They were assigned farm tasks equal to their strength and abilities. *Signore* Mandaro asked me to join him on the rear *portico* of his facility. It was a tranquil location, a nice place to talk.

"*Signor* Mandaro, what do you feel are the essential concerns that must be addressed for any person to succeed as a salesperson?"

After a brief pause to gather his thoughts, he responded. "Giuseppe, first, you must have a product that you can believe in, one that is of the highest quality, one that provides a significant amount of value for the price charged. To start, let me explain how I grew my business with quality products, then backed it up with outstanding service. Giuseppe, over twenty-nine years ago when I first started making cheese, I always looked for anyone who would try a sample piece. I knew once they tried it, they would recognize the quality and buy. If they wanted to use the cheese in a pasta dish, like lasagna, I would help them envision how good the finished dish would taste. I pointed out that their family and guests would compliment them on their cooking skills. By combining all the ingredients, including our fresh cheeses and their skills, they would make a pan of lasagna which would make them very proud. Then, as a sign of our commitment, I would say, 'If you are not satisfied with our cheese, I will refund what you paid for it.' Pepe, I have had a money return policy as long as I have been in business, and I never once had to return the price of any purchase."

> ◌◈◌
> *First, you must have a product that you can believe in, one that is of the highest quality, one that provides a significant amount of value for the price charged.*
> ◌◈◌

"But, *Signor* Mandaro, how can your success relate to fabrics and the House of Pesce?"

"Pepe, in your business you want potential buyers to see and feel the quality of the fabrics. You want them to envision the fabric as part of a tapestry that would hang in a cathedral, or the *palazzo della ragione*, the town square; or perhaps a beautiful silk fabric that your grandfather imports from China, as an attractive gown for a lovely woman."

"Did you like the dress that your sister, Marie Angela, wore at Vincenzo's dance recital?"

> CBEO
> *Delivering a believable presentation is at the heart of the selling process. It starts with believing that you are offering the best. Next, is getting your customer to believe the same thing.*
> CBEO

"*Si, Signor* Mandaro, it was very attractive. In fact, she looked beautiful in it. Mother and *Zia* Catherine did a wonderful job making it."

Signore Mandaro continued. "If you were selling the material to your mother, your approach would not focus on the fabric—the texture, durability, type of yarn, and so on, although that might be important to some. The real appeal to the purchaser would be how the *finished product* benefits them and those that will use, wear, or otherwise enjoy the product. When you show your fabrics, you must show the benefits to your customer. Delivering a believable presentation is at the heart of the selling process. It starts with believing that you are offering the best. Next, is getting your customer to believe the same thing. You have spoken with the *Monsignore*, yes?"

"*Si*, he spoke of knowledge and building relationships."

"*Bene*, Pepe, building relationships is the most important of all skills of the successful sales master. Mutually trusting relationships will help you pinpoint the needs of your customers. Your biggest responsibility, after establishing a trusting, believable relationship, is to help customers pinpoint problem areas. Get your customer to feel comfortable enough to freely discuss his interests and problems. Only after the customer agrees that there is something wanted or needed can you proceed. The House of Pesce offers many varieties of fabrics, correct?"

I nodded and scribbled in my Chronicles as fast as I could.

"Having more than one product to discuss is a tremendous benefit because it gives you the opportunity to offer your customer multiple alternatives—all yours. As you discuss one product at a time, gauge your customer's interest by the questions asked, the comments, and the interest shown. If one product is not appealing, try others. If you put a sample in the customer's hand, the customer is forced to look at and inspect the item. The quality of Pesce fabrics can be seen, felt, and appreciated. By having the fabric in their hands, customers can understand more fully the many qualities that you will talk about. Now, Pepe, you have gotten to a point where your customer wants to know more. Thus, you must learn as much as possible about your customers before you meet them in order to serve them better. This is done by becoming familiar with their wants and desires. Are you reviewing that with your grandfather?"

> ☙❧
> *Having more than one product to discuss is a tremendous benefit because it gives you the opportunity to offer your customer multiple alternatives— all yours.*
> ☙❧

"*Si, Signor* Mandaro. I am."

"*Bene.* Now, Giuseppe, I must go back to the shop. Do you feel that I have helped you?"

"*Si, Signor* Mandaro, *grazie.* I appreciate your time and what you have told me. *Arrivederci.*"

Key Points in My Chronicles

⊖ By providing outstanding service, coupled with a strong belief in my products, I will face competitors. If practical, I will give customers a sample of my product to try. I will conduct a complete demonstration so they can appreciate the quality of my product.

⊖ The probability of a sale goes up when customers envision the enjoyment of owning my products and realize the many benefits and value of my service. I want to give them a sense of ownership.

⊖ By building a long-term, trusting relationship with customers, I create a credibility that should be able to withstand an occasional mistake. I will continually remind customers of the many benefits and values they receive when buying from me. I will not stop selling just because they are customers.

⊖ I will try to get every customer to buy every one of my products that they can use. It is easier to sell additional products in my line after I get the first order. Getting additional business from a customer is easier than getting a new customer.

CHAPTER 11

The Rabbi Comes to the Church

Sales Lessons From a King

That night I went to visit the *Monsignore* again, and as we were enjoying one of *Signora* Silipigni's wonderful biscottis, there was a rap on the study door. Without waiting for a reply, a head appeared.

"*Buona sera, Monsignore*, and to you Master Pesce, how are you gentlemen this evening?"

"*Bene, bene*," the *Monsignore* replied for both of us. I did not know the stranger, but it was obvious that he knew my name. "Rabbi, let me introduce my long-time friend. I have known him since he was born and his family for over thirty years. Rabbi Guido Santucci, this is Giuseppe Vincenzo Pesce, the grandson of the fabrics dealer, *Signore* Vincenzo Pesce, the founder and patriarch of the House of Pesce."

"Rabbi?" was all I could utter as my jaw dropped. I had read a little about Jews at the monastery, but I never thought there would be one, a rabbi, a real Jew, here in Florence. Here in a church. Here in the *Monsignore's* study. Here talking to me!

The *Monsignore* noticed my shock and quickly explained.

"The Rabbi leads a small group of Jews here in Florence who have been in hiding for many years." The *Monsignore* continued, "When a new pope is installed, the politics involved not only disturb the Catholic community, but send shock waves into the Jewish population as well." The *Monsignore* felt he needed to explain further.

"Pepe, occasionally local Papal representatives, and those from Rome, go on an excursion attempting to 'purge the flock,' as it is called. What a disgrace on the church. We know it is written in the Old Testament that the Jews are the chosen people, yet there are some who persecute them. When will there be peace and harmony in this world? Rabbi Santucci immigrated here from Rome many years ago and has mostly kept his activities very secret. You know his brother, Enrico. He is one of your grandfather's most trusted employees. I have known the Rabbi since I was a seminary student studying in Rome, over forty years ago. At the time, Rome was more tolerant towards Jews, and Rabbi Santucci and his family were able to enjoy a relatively peaceful existence."

"His father was a stone mason and helped to build many of the fountains and churches in Rome. He also helped in building the Piazza del Mucato Vicclio, the fountain in Florence at the exact center of the city."

The Rabbi asked, "And what is your trade, Master Pesce?"

"I am a sales apprentice," I answered meekly.

"What?"

"A sales apprentice," I repeated, apparently this time even more meekly.

"Giuseppe, why are you talking so softly? Are you not proud to be a sales apprentice?" asked the Rabbi.

"Actually, Rabbi Santucci, I am not pleased with my efforts as a sales apprentice. I am not certain if I will ever become a sales master. I sometimes feel that Almighty God has another trade meant for me."

"Nonsense," said the *Monsignore*. "You can do very well as a sales apprentice if you continue to follow the training of your grandfather and his associates and follow the principles written in the Holy Scriptures."

"Yes, the Scriptures," the Rabbi chimed in, "They contain one message after another giving positive encouragement."

"One example is in the Psalms written by David," the *Monsignore* began. "David was a shepherd boy who became a king. His 23rd Psalm will give you encouragement. Let me explain." The *Monsignore* enjoyed teaching about the Bible and started to dissect and explain the Psalm. "'The Lord is my Shepherd; I shall not want.' (Ps. 23:1) David's knowledge of shepherding was unsurpassed. He was very familiar with the demands placed on a shepherd to locate food and water for his flock, both of which were scarce in the parched land. David had to know his territory. Giuseppe, you must do the same thing. You must know your territory and who would be interested in your products and services."

> ***You must know your territory and who would be interested in your products and services.***

The *Monsignore* continued, "'He makes me to lie down in green pastures. He leads me beside the still waters. He restores my soul; He leads me in the paths of righteousness for His name's sake.' (Ps. 23:2,3) David knew of the few underground springs hidden in the rocky crevices of the wilderness. There he would lead his sheep to the pools of fresh water where they could drink and be restored. Giuseppe, if you become exhausted in your travels, you must rest and refresh your body so you will be restored in mind and spirit.

Pepe, it was not uncommon for shepherds to spend the night with the flock out in the hills. The high mountain cliffs totally blocked the sunlight, causing dark ravines where the shepherd and his flock would be found. David recalls these frightful moments when he and his flock were easy prey for wild leopards, lions, and bears. 'Yea, though I walk through the valley of the shadow of death, I will fear no evil; for You are with me; Your rod and Your staff, they comfort me.' (Ps. 23:4) David's reference to a physical fear as a child adds an even greater spiritual meaning to his Psalm of praise.

"'You prepare a table before me in the presence of my enemies; You anoint my head with oil; my cup runs over." (Ps. 23:5) The *Monsignore* continued, "A noted practice of David's day was to break bread—or eat a meal together—as a covenant of peace, security, and forgiveness. Here, David acknowledges that God makes peace with his enemies. God anoints his head with oil as a sign of His blessing. His cup running over signifies the success and prosperity God bestowed upon him.

"The Psalm reflects a beautiful relationship between David and his Lord, for David saw God at work in the ordinary daily activities of life. His Psalm of comfort and praise can also be our own as we realize God's gifts of security, peace, and prosperity in our lives. Then we can also say with David, 'Surely goodness and mercy shall follow me all the days of my life; and I will dwell in the house of the Lord forever.'" (Ps. 23:6)

> ✑
> *My son, you will do well as a sales apprentice and continue as a sales master if you follow the words that you are entering in your Chronicles and follow the words in the Scriptures.*
> ✑

The *Monsignore* looked at the Rabbi and then at me. He said to me, "My son, you will do well as a sales apprentice and continue as a sales master if you follow the words that you are entering in your Chronicles and the words in the Scriptures."

The Rabbi asked if I would like to visit him sometime soon and talk more about life on the road as a sales apprentice. He said many members of his congregation were in the merchandising business and that he had observed some ideas listening to them. He thought they might be helpful. I thanked him for his offer and said I would be pleased to visit him. We set a meeting date as I bid the Rabbi and the *Monsignore* good night.

Key Points in My Chronicles

- ⊖ I will be proud of the sales profession. By introducing new products and services to an ever-demanding public, I am helping people to get more of what they want out of life.

- ⊖ I will listen to all those who can help with my sales training. Ideas and guidance in my development will come from many sources, including the inspirational messages written in God's words.

- ⊖ My customers will know I believe in God and see the depth of my faith by my actions.

- ⊖ I will commit all of my talents and energies to the glory of God. They are from Him.

CHAPTER 12

I Go to See Rabbi Santucci

The Value of Sales Planning and the Need for Humor

As I walked to Rabbi Guido Santucci's, I considered his position. He was a man of God, but like none I had met before. I was looking forward to the meeting. The Rabbi came to the door when I knocked. We greeted each other with a traditional Italian hug. He is a very warm and sensitive person. His face, although appearing very calm, showed the signs of anxiety caused by the frequent verbal and sometimes physical harm inflicted on him and other Jews. A small group of radical Florentines were guilty of these vicious attacks. It was a disgrace to the city.

With the frequent changes in the hierarchy of the Catholic Church over the last fifty years, there was not a consistent denouncement of these attacks. Often, if the population in a region wanted to befriend and align themselves with the Catholic clergy, they would harass members of the Jewish community. The Rabbi had withstood all these attacks. It was obvious that he was a very godly man. His friend, *Monsignore* Mazza, was a unique member of the Catholic clergy because he frequently invited the Rabbi over for dinner or a quiet night to discuss the classics in Latin or Greek. The Rabbi and his small flock of followers were well-liked and respected by the majority of Florentines.

The Rabbi knew of my plight and my training as a sales apprentice. It seemed the whole city of Florence heard about Giuseppe Pesce and the troubles he was having filling his father's shoes. Grandfather apparently did not need Johann Gutenberg's printing press to spread the word.

"Giuseppe, I have been talking to some friends about how to become a sales master, and I have picked up a few suggestions for you. As you know, there is nothing I would like more than to see you achieve success for yourself and the House of Pesce."

"Rabbi, God bless you, I can use all the suggestions and help possible. Working with my grandfather, I am developing a book of ideas and suggestions that I call my Chronicles. Every time I talk to someone who has an idea or I identify information that could help me, I am recording that information in the Chronicles. Many people are anxious to support me, and I appreciate your wisdom."

The Rabbi was very willing to help because he had a sincere interest in me and he wanted to show his appreciation for my grandfather's generosity. I knew Grandfather frequently sent bolts of fabric to the Rabbi. They were always our finest silks from China. Grandfather said it was for the glory of God. The Rabbi told Grandfather that he used the fabrics to make tapestries to adorn the small room where he held Sabbath and holiday services. The finest silk, made with gold thread, was used to make the covering cloth for the Torah. The Rabbi was very proud to be a friend of Vincenzo Pesce. I am sure Grandfather felt the same way about the Rabbi.

"Pepe," the Rabbi continued, "let me mention a few key points that I know will help you as you go down the road to becoming a successful person and sales master. You must have a goal, a plan. It should be for a long period of time. A long-term goal will reduce the discouragement of short-range problems and failures; it will help you keep your eye on the mark."

After a brief pause, he picked up the Bible that the Monsignore had given him and found the place he wanted. "In your Bible, as well as in Jewish writings, it is written that there is an appointed time for everything. Here it is in the third verse of Ecclesiastes. It says, 'To everything there is a season, a time for every purpose under the heaven, a time to weep, and a time to laugh.'" He stopped quoting and added, "Remember this verse in your planning and in handling the rejections you will receive from customers. It will help when you consider that certain things take time—everything having its time and place, even the unwelcome rejections. Also, it mentions having a time to laugh. Pepe, you must develop a sense of wit and humor."

> ☙
> *You must have a goal, a plan. A long-term goal will reduce the discouragement of short-range problems and failures; it will help you keep your eye on the mark.*
> ☙

"Humor, Rabbi? How does that help me?"

The Rabbi was anxious to explain. "Humor is like grease that you put on the axle of your wagon. It helps you function smoothly. I believe Almighty God realized there would be problems that mere mortals like us could do nothing about, and that we must learn how to live through them. I am sure God gave us laughter as a relief for the tension we experience as we go through life. Good humor is the best antidote for discouragement. It helps rid your mind of anxiety and depression. It gives us serenity and contentment. Finally, know that God is in charge, and watches all of our actions. Those who God knows through their faith can be confident He is putting everything in their lives together for their good."

After another pause, he went on. "Pepe, know that God has a plan for you and that the plan is good. Keep a sense of humor in the midst of your trials. Make long-term goals for your selling with specific plans to help you reach those goals. If you do this, you will grow as a sales apprentice."

"Rabbi, is the Torah really the Old Testament?"

"Yes, Pepe, the Torah is part of your Old Testament. Or as we Jews say, your Old Testament is part of the Torah. Like your Bible, it is full of inspirational verses. Most of it was written by Moses. It contains the first five parts of your Old Testament. It goes from Genesis to Deuteronomy, with Exodus, Leviticus and Numbers in between."

> ೞ೦
> **Be strong and resolute, be not in fear or dread for the Lord your God Himself marches with you. He will not fail you or forsake you.**
> ೞ೦

"Thank you, Rabbi. I appreciate your words. Is there anything in your Scripture, the Torah, that can inspire me the same way?"

"*Si*, Pepe, there is much. In the last book, Deuteronomy, Moses was in his last days and wrote: 'Be strong and resolute, be not in fear or in dread, for the Lord your God Himself marches with you. He will not fail you or forsake you.'" Handing me a folded parchment sheet, the Rabbi said, "Here, Giuseppe, I wrote these inspirational words on a piece of parchment for you. Take it and read it many times during the day. When you memorize it, continue to repeat the words. They will give you strength and encouragement."

I read them again before I left. I thanked the Rabbi for his time and commented that I had two inspirational verses to remember and wonderful information for my Chronicles. It was an exhilarating evening.

Key Points in My Chronicles

⊖ Having my goals in writing will help me over-come temporary setbacks and rejections. A written goal is an ideal reference.

⊖ A sense of humor is the antidote for discourage-ment. I will always take what I do seriously, but I will laugh at myself when I make a mistake. I will strive not to repeat mistakes.

⊖ Winners get up at least one more time than they are knocked down. Persistence prevails when all else fails.

⊖ Almighty God has a plan for me, and it is a good plan. I will set aside quiet times during the day, and particularly at night, to listen to and reflect on His plans for my life.

⊖ Everyone wants to be with positive, joyful people. I will strive to make everyone, particu-larly customers, pleased that we have met.

CHAPTER 13

$\mathcal{U}$ncle $\mathcal{G}$iovanni $\mathcal{T}$alks About $\mathcal{S}$ales $\mathcal{T}$echniques

The Importance of Emphasizing Benefits to the Customer

isiting *Zio* Giovanni and *Zia* Catherine, my uncle and aunt, was always fun. They did not have any children, and our families have always been close. Not only was my father *Zio's* brother, but my mother was Aunt Catherine's sister. Two brothers married two sisters. Since my father's death, they have tried to fill the void. No one could replace my father, but God bless them, they did everything possible.

Uncle Giovanni is very smart. Years ago, he studied at the universities in Rome and Pisa and is now generally regarded as one of the most respected legal minds in all of the Republic of

Florence. He often presented significant matters before the tribunal. This was my second opportunity to visit Uncle Giovanni and talk about salesmanship. When I last saw him, he said there were still a few areas he wanted to discuss with me. So I returned at the time he suggested, for dinner, a few days later.

"Pepe, let us discuss a few attitudes you must have for success in sales. One is desire. In Latin it is *desiderare.* Desire is having a strong craving or longing for something; a wish; a request. You must want what you seek. In sales, what you seek is typically an order. Another requirement for your success is persistence. In Latin, *persistentem* means 'not falling off, or continuing in the face of opposition.' For you, this means not accepting a customer's rejection as a personal commentary. It means that you must try again."

He checked my reaction, then went on. "Empathy is the third attitude, and it comes from the Greek *en* and *pathos* meaning 'in feeling.' It is your ability to share in another's emotions, thoughts or feelings. In addition, Pepe, I want to discuss a skill that will come in very handy for you as you attempt to persuade customers to buy fabrics from the House of Pesce.

"We will talk about these things after supper. Come, *Zia* Catherine is waiting for us to have dinner. She has a very special meal—*gnocchi* with marinara sauce and sausage."

Aunt Catherine's *gnocchi* and sauce is one of my favorite meals. The *gnocchi,* made with fresh mashed potatoes mixed with flour, egg, salt and pepper, plus a touch of garlic, was rolled out and cut into small pieces about the size of a grape. Then they were cooked, drained, and served with the tasty marinara sauce and topped with some of *Signore* Mandaro's parmesan cheese.

After dinner we went outside to continue my sales training. As we walked through the gardens, we stopped at a statue that had a masonry bench in front of it. We sat down facing the statue. Uncle said it was a statue of the Goddess Maat, the symbol of the legal profession, a blindfolded lady holding the scales of justice.

"*Zio*, the lady is blindfolded so that she will be impartial in her decision and that the scales will tip and the balance swayed based on the facts that are presented without any prejudice. Correct?"

"*Si*, Pepe, but this scale is also a valuable symbol that you can use to help yourself as you continue your training."

"Uncle Giovanni, I remember we talked about the scales when I was here last. How can the scales help me in my sales training?"

"Let us think about it, Giuseppe Pesce, young sales apprentice for the House of Pesce. The scales represent a balance, and the two dishes are intended to hold weights so one side can be equated against the other. Do you notice in the market that many shops have these balance scales, and the merchants place food items on one side and small weights on the other side?"

> *In addition to the experiences you are gathering yourself, we want to help you by sharing the experiences of others.*

"*Si*, Uncle, I am familiar with how they weigh items, and then the shopkeeper charges accordingly."

"Well, Pepe, that same principal of weights and balances is an important one for you to learn as a sales apprentice. Let me give you a few examples. Let us imagine that you are in a new town calling on a merchant whom you have not done business with before. Would you call that a difficult situation?"

"*Si*, Uncle, calling on a new merchant is very difficult. It makes me very discouraged. Last week, I had such a poor trip in the territory that when I returned home I took my wagon off the road so Grandfather would not hear me come in."

"I know, Pepe . . . and when you were off the road the axle on the wagon broke. I know."

"How did you find out?"

"Pepe, my Pepe, your grandfather and I know the struggles you are facing. Papa faced them when he started in business, and he helped your father as he started in the territory as a sales apprentice. You are learning through experience, and sometimes the price is high. Now, in addition to the experiences you are gathering yourself, we want to help you by sharing the experiences of others. Experiences that you have and experiences that others have, if they are relevant, are all opportunities for you to learn. Although I am not a sales master, my knowledge of the House of Pesce and of the scales of balance can help in your training. It could be that the person you are trying to sell to does not know you, your products, or your reputation. Visualize that the weights he places on the competitor's side must be counterbalanced on the other side by weights that you add."

Uncle Giovanni continued, "Your weights, Pepe, are the benefits and values they receive from doing business with you. You must make the customer feel comfortable and confident in you and your wares. Before a merchant will discuss your wares, and definitely before he will buy, he first must buy you!"

It could be that the person you are trying to sell to does not know you, your products, or your reputation. Visualize that the weights he places on the competitor's side must be counter-balanced on the other side by weights that you add.

"Buy me, Uncle Giovanni? Buy me? What do you mean, Uncle?"

"Pepe, new merchants must first trust you. They will form an opinion early in your meeting. This opinion, when favorable, will make them feel comfortable in listening to your discussion about your wares. Then they may trust you and believe you. Then you can proceed with an opportunity to make a sale."

Assume you are calling on a merchant customer for the first time, and consider our scales of balance. On one side of the scale you can visualize the merchant placing a weight for each concern he has.

"Uncle, on a first call, how do I make a merchant trust me and believe me? This is our initial meeting."

"My nephew, trust starts with your approach and continues until a decision is made and after. Giuseppe, before you approach a merchant's shop, stop your wagon several meters from the threshold. Get off, dust off your sandals, make certain that your cloak is neat, wipe the dirt from your face, put your hair in order, and ensure the painted sign on the wagon is clean. Check your fabric samples. Are they clean? Are loose threads clipped? Do you know the price of each bolt? Approach with a positive gait and an enthusiastic smile. With eyes wide open say, '*Buon giorno*, my name is Giuseppe Pesce, representing the House of Pesce, the largest manufacturer and distributor of fabrics in Florence. It would be a pleasure to show you our fine line.' Then with a pleasant smile on your face, while handing a swatch of your fabrics say, 'Is this not an attractive pattern? Would this not be ideal for one of your customers?'" He paused, then continued. "Giuseppe, once the merchant sees that you are another businessman with a positive, enthusiastic approach, he will be more inclined to listen to you. As he listens, he will quickly build trust."

"I understand, Uncle, and this positive approach is like adding a weight to my side of the scale."

"*Si*, now what are some of the other weights you can use to tip the scales in your favor? Let us list them, Pepe, because these should all go into your Chronicles."

"Well, I can mention many of the other fine merchants who buy our fabrics. I can refer to the members of the Medici family who wear garments made from our fabrics, and also the many tapestries we have hanging in museums, public buildings and the cathedrals in Florence, Milan, and Naples. I could also mention that the garments and vestments worn by dignitaries in business, government, and the clergy were all made from the House of Pesce fabrics."

> ⧉
> *Once the merchant sees that you are another business man with a positive, enthusiastic approach, he will be more inclined to listen to you . . . he will quickly build trust.*
> ⧉

"Giuseppe, you also need to show customers how, by purchasing from you, they receive many benefits. These are the weights I talk about. Do you recognize how this approach can help you?"

"*Si, Zio* Giovanni, this approach is one I will use. I see where the sales master must always mention additional values and benefits delivered so the customers visualize receiving more than they pay. Uncle, when I talk about customer benefits, it is like the advantage of our pigeon delivery system. Grandfather said he was going to explain more about how he got started using the pigeons, but there was something else that I was curious about."

"What would you like to know, Pepe?"

"Uncle, it has been said that at one time grandfather placed a wager of one hundred florins with *Signore* Medici and won. It was on a race with their pigeons."

"Oh, the alleged pigeon bet between grandfather and *Signore* Medici?" Without taking a breath he continued, "Do you think that my father, your grandfather, the patriarch of the House of Pesce, a devout church-goer and upstanding citizen of Florence, would make a bet, a wager? My Pepe, how could you think that? Do not waste your time talking about such idle gossip, you have many more important matters to address as you pursue your sales career."

He saw my hesitancy.

"If, hypothetically, grandfather did race against *Signore* Medici's flock, it apparently ended with no ill feelings because the Medicis are some of grandfather's best friends. Enough about bets! You get back to thinking about being a sales master."

Uncle went on to say that when grandfather flies his birds outside of the immediate area, he always puts a small strip of leather on one leg with the markings of the House of Pesce, a fish in a circle. If the birds ever stray and land in another pigeon coop, that person will recognize grandfather's symbol and return it. Grandfather always gives the person a handsome reward.

"Now, Giuseppe, you should go home to relax. Give my regards to your family."

"*Ciao*, Uncle."

As we walked towards the house from the gardens, I thought of all that I had learned. When we reached the house, I hugged my aunt and uncle, thanked them and went home. It had been a very fruitful visit. That evening I had received a double blessing, a delicious meal prepared by *Zia* Catherine to fill my stomach and valuable information from *Zio* Giovanni to fill my mind.

Key Points in My Chronicles

⊖ The balance scales can help me visualize my relationship with the customer. I must present the customer with enough benefits on the "buy" side to outweigh any negatives on the "do not buy" side.

⊖ I must keep introducing values and benefits to tip the scales in the customer's favor. I will not discuss price until I am sure that the customer realizes that the values I present are important.

⊖ My attitude is extremely important to my success. Attitudes are the looking glass to my soul. They reflect what makes me different from every other person in the world.

⊖ Three attitudes I must always demonstrate are desire, persistence, and empathy.

⊖ I cannot change my past; I cannot change the fact that people will act in a certain way; I cannot change the inevitable. The only thing I can do is play on the one string I have, and that is my attitude. I am in charge of my attitude. I will always remember that "If it is to be, it is up to me."

CHAPTER 14

Mother Talks About Life, the Masters, and Selling

Dealing with Diversity, Having a Vision, and Persistence

During the week I had many opportunities to talk to Mother about the information I had been collecting for my Chronicles. I knew the information and guidance that I received from *Signore* Bugatti and *Signore* Mandaro, as well as the inspirational messages that I heard from *Monsignore* Mazza and Rabbi Santucci, would serve me well. I planned to follow their counsel.

On Thursday, Marie Angela left home late in the morning. She went to take a picnic lunch to Vincenzo while he rehearsed with the dance troupe. The practice hall was adjacent to the conservatory studio that was used by many of the masters and apprentices who were plying their artistic talents in Florence. The area was a central location for artists of all types.

Marie Angela enjoyed visiting the studio area at mid-day, the time when the dancers and other artisans and apprentices took their lunch break. They strolled in the plaza in front of their buildings and typically relaxed and had a bite to eat. Marie Angela, although knowing that Vincenzo ate very little during rehearsals, took enough fruit, cheese, and bread for three. As Vincenzo knew—and the family suspected—she was hoping to see an apprentice painter and sculptor named Michelangelo Buonarroti. Mamma always smiled as she helped pack the picnic lunch basket.

Marie Angela always set her hair and wore a very attractive dress when she brought lunch for Vincenzo. By having extra food, it was easy for her to ask Master Buonarroti if he would like to join her and Vincenzo for a light picnic lunch. Marie Angela, during this time in her life, was rather shy and would have thought it too forward to approach Michelangelo without a good reason. Food in Florence was always a good reason to open a conversation. It worked for Marie Angela, particularly with Vincenzo being a willing accomplice on her mission to be with Master Michelangelo Buonarroti.

Marie Angela first met Michelangelo Buonarroti when he was studying under the watchful eye of Domenico Ghirlandaio, who was, at the time, the most popular painter in all of Florence. Michelangelo studied with him for two years before he began studying sculpture and living in the Palazzo Medici. I think Michelangelo liked Marie Angela, because he told her a story that was fairly widespread but not many people knew if it was true. Michelangelo told Marie Angela that part of his training as a sculptor was the tough task of cutting stone. *Signore* Lorenzo di Pierfrancesco, his tutor, assigned him the challenge of chiseling a scrap piece of marble into an old fawn. *Signore* di Pierfrancesco, taking a look at Michelangelo's first attempt, said that such an old fawn could not possibly have such a complete set of teeth.

Michelangelo corrected the situation forthwith. With one blow of his chisel he knocked out a tooth in the upper jaw. That decisiveness endeared him to *Signore* Pierfrancesco, who knew he was dealing with a potential master. At that time, the community of Florence artisans and patrons did not know the full genius of the master in training, Michelangelo.

Mother frequently talked to Marie Angela about the artists and others of different races whom she would meet on her visits to see Vincenzo. One day when I was home, I heard Mother talk about what she referred to as "diversity." Mother explained that it meant different, contrasting. She said that as I pursue my career in sales, I must be comfortable associating with individuals who come from different countries and speak different languages. Their skin may be a different color than ours, and they may practice a different religion, but she said we are all children of God, and we should never prejudge anyone because of these differences.

> ♋♋
> *Look at individuals not by the color of their skin, or the language they speak or where they come from, but look at them based on who they are and how you relate to them.*
> ♋♋

Mother said, "Marie Angela, do you see the masters inviting fledgling artists with different skin colors and different religions to study at their studios and academies? Many of them even dress very differently than you and Giuseppe. Do you not think that unusually creative people frequently use their clothes as an outward sign of their individuality? Even Vincenzo dresses different than Giuseppe. Or look at the painter, Leonardo da Vinci. He is very different. It is said he has a temper and does not finish all his projects. It is also said that he does not know what he is—a painter, an architect, a sculptor or an engineer. Some say he had a relationship with Madonna Elisabetta, the wife of Franceso del Giocondo, for whom he was painting a portrait which he called the Mona Lisa."

"Mother, Leonardo da Vinci may be one of the most brilliant artists in all of Florence, perhaps all of Italy."

"My children, that is exactly what I am talking about. Look at individuals not by the color of their skin, or the language they speak or where they come from, but look at them based on who they are and how you relate to them. Does not Grandfather buy from merchants who come from China? Is their skin not of a yellow hue? Does he not buy from merchants who bring very colorful fabrics from Africa, and is their skin not dark brown?"

Mother had our attention, so she continued. "There are some who have trouble understanding and believing all the precepts of the Roman Catholic Church; they are concerned with the power that Rome exerts in everything we do. They are protesting, so we call them Protestants. We may not agree with them, but we should always recognize their rights. We are all children of God."

Marie Angela chimed in with, "Yes, mother, I see where society is becoming more and more diverse. What we see in Florence is only a small cross section of the activities going on in Venice, Naples, Milan, Rome, and all of Italy. Just as grandfather, who is a generation older than you, looks for the best in people and strives for a rewarding and mutually enjoyable relationship with those of different cultures, we must be receptive to others and not be harsh on those who are different from us."

"That is right. You, Giuseppe, and Vincenzo must look at a situation from a stranger's eyes. What would they say because you are different from them? Should they fear you? Of course, not. You want others, even if they are different, to be your friends." Mother wanted to talk about Michelangelo, the young man in whom Marie Angela appeared to have an interest.

"Marie Angela, what does this Michelangelo tell you about this sculpture he is working on, particularly regarding the block of Carrara marble that is at the cathedral? It has been said that it is so large and irregular that many think nothing good could possibly come from it. The marble is so awkward and big that they are calling it *Il gigante*, the Giant. Does he say that he is wasting his time, and is he simply taking the money of the *Operai* Guild, who commissioned him for the statue? Do you think he is taking advantage of those who trust him?"

"No, Mother. Michelangelo, like all good artists, has a vision that must be followed with persistence, just as Giuseppe must have vision and persistence as he goes out into the territory. *Mama mia*, those were two key traits that you said my father had. He worked hard as a peddler salesman for grandfather because he always wanted to give the best to you and us children. You knew it was hard being alone with us when Father was in the territory; however, you had the vision to recognize that as the business of the House of Pesce grew, there would be more time for Father to stay in Florence and be with us."

"Mama, Grandfather and Grandmother Pesce say you are an exceptional woman. They say they pray for us every day. Papa says if it were not for your support, encouragement, and your ability to show our father the value of visualizing a goal and having the perseverance to achieve it, he would not have enjoyed the success he did as a sales master."

Mother's face grew solemn, and Marie Angela changed the subject. Mother always became sad when reminded of her loving husband.

"*Mama mia*, the large piece of marble that Michelangelo is working on will someday be a work of art. He visualizes it being admired and accepted by the *Operai* Guild, and that it will be placed on public display on the platform of the Plaza Vecchio. He already knows that upon completing that big piece of marble you call *Il Gigante,* it will become the statue of the Biblical king, David. He thinks it will someday be revered by many peoples of all cultures.

"As he accurately strikes each blow and the chips fall to the floor, he visualizes each unneeded piece and gets ready for the next blow. Michelangelo said that when he first saw the discarded, awkward piece of marble, he immediately visualized the statue inside that he would find. He knew he had to persistently chip away, a piece at a time, until he found it."

> CɜƐꝹ
> *Michelangelo would make a beautiful statue from an unusual, rejected piece of stone because he could visualize what he was looking for inside the marble and make his vision a reality—chip by chip, blow by blow.*
> CƷꝪꙄ

As I wrote in my Chronicles, I contemplated our discussions. Mother, Marie Angela, and I had a wonderful time talking about topics that will help us as we grow in our business and personal life. I realized that Michelangelo would make a beautiful statue from an unusual, rejected piece of stone because he could visualize what he was looking for inside the marble and make his vision a reality—chip by chip, blow by blow. Visualization and persistence were Michelangelo's driving forces. They would be mine as well.

Key Points in My Chronicles

———— ⟨⟩ ————

⊖ I will accept people for who they are and what they do. I will never judge a customer by looks alone. I will take the time and make the effort to get to know them.

⊖ My objectives must be written down. When I just keep a vision in my mind, it is not really a goal; it is only a dream.

⊖ I will strive to make my vision a reality through a series of action steps that take me from where I am now to where I want to be.

⊖ Continually striving for self-improvement is the mark of the sales master.

CHAPTER 15

Grandfather Discusses Personal Growth

The Need for Continual Improvement

The next morning I went to visit Grandfather to discuss some of the many new things I had learned. Grandfather was in his garden, so I waited for him to return.

Grandfather and Grandmother Pesce had a wonderful home. Grandmother's curtains, wall decorations, and furniture coverings were always the best available from the House of Pesce. When she heard that new fabrics were arriving, she would visit the warehouse. She would go, knowing exactly how much material she required for each article she wanted to make. Federico would escort her through the warehouse, pointing out the newest fabrics as she made her selections. He would then cut the amount required and deliver it personally. Later, Grandmother, my mother, and Aunt Catherine would all help in sewing the new curtains, tapestries, and furniture coverings. The whole family was proud of my grandparents' home.

When Grandmother did not like some of the new fabrics, she would ask, "Federico, did *Signore* Pesce have his glasses on when he selected this one?" or "Did he pay for this ugly fabric, or was it given as a complimentary sample?" Federico, being the consummate politician, would frequently respond with a nonre-criminating answer: "*Signora* Pesce, maybe *Signore* Pesce was out visiting a customer when the fabric selection was made, possibly by one of his assistants, or perhaps it was selected by your grand-daughter, Marie Angela. She has been selecting some of our fastest selling new products." He was a master at protecting my Grandfa-ther from any unpleasant situations. He would add, "*Signora* Pesce, it is sometimes hard to select fabrics and predict the wide range of tastes of our customers. Some fabrics that we buy on speculation in very small quantities turn out to have wide appeal, and we have to reorder very quickly. You select what you would like to have in your lovely home, and it will be my pleasure to cut and deliver it personally."

When Grandmother came to visit the facility, Grandfather would often tease her saying, "Carolina, how come you only decide to bring me lunch when you know I have new goods? Do you not concern yourself with my meals at other times?" Grand-mother, never at a loss for words, would smile and say, "Oh, my wonderful husband, of course I concern myself about you every day, but I feel if I come over more frequently, you may want to give me an extra kiss on my cheek, and that would be a distrac-tion to you and all the employees of the House of Pesce. I think it best that I come over only on an occasional visit. Do you not like to see me, Vincenzo?" It appeared obvious that Grandmother had learned the salesmanship and persuasion tactics of Grandfa-ther, my father, and my uncle, because she frequently ended her responses with another question.

"My Carolina, you are welcome to visit me at any time, and, of course, when you do not come, you always send Marie Angela over with my lunch, *grazie*." With a big smile, he continued. "*Bella mia*, after you make your selections with Federico, while he cuts the fabric, please come in the office, and maybe I will draw the curtains and put out the 'do not disturb' sign. What do you think?"

"I think you need to go back to work, Vincenzo," she said as she headed for the door. Grandmother enjoyed her visits to the warehouse, seeing all the activity, but she enjoyed it more when she was leading the activity, especially in the kitchen.

As Grandfather approached from the garden, I waved and called out for him, "Papa, Papa, *buon giorno,* Papa, I have learned so much this week. I feel I know everything necessary to be successful as a sales master!"

"My son, you can never be totally satisfied with your present situation as it relates to your performance as a sales apprentice. You must always look for ways to improve. You must strive to do better tomorrow than today. My son, the real sign of a master, whether in the arts or in commerce, is having a certain amount of dissatisfaction."

I interrupted, "Dissatisfaction, Papa? Why should I, a salesman, be dissatisfied, particularly if I am successful?"

"Giuseppe, sales masters are professionals. They have reached a high level of competency. However, the driving force that keeps them performing at the highest levels is the goal of always doing better. They always look for the perfect painting, the perfect sculpture, the perfect poem or, indeed, the perfect sale. Improvement will come if you follow three simple steps. First, your must decide what you want. I mean, you must have a goal and a strong desire to reach a certain level. Write down your goal. This gives you focus. Second, you must decide what you are willing to give up to get it."

> 附
> *Improvement will come if you follow three simple steps. First, you must decide what you want. . . . Second, you must decide what you are willing to give up to get it. . . . The last step is getting into action by doing what is necessary.*
> 附

"But, Papa, why must I give up something in order to reach my goals?"

"Well, Pepe, if you are not achieving what you desire now, it means that you are not doing something right. You must eliminate the things that get in the way of achieving your goals. In selling, this may include: not asking the right questions, or not asking for the order, or not making a good presentation, or not having proper discipline—that is, not being disciplined enough to make the calls required. Or, it could mean not answering a customer's questions or concerns. Pepe, do you understand some of the undesirable things you must give up to get what you want?"

"Yes, Grandfather, I can see that after setting goals, I must give up something to reach them. You mentioned there were three steps to reach them, Papa. What is the third?"

"The last step is getting into action by doing what is necessary. You have heard me use the word motivation. The root of the word motivation is *moto*, which means 'movement' or 'action.' This is the driving force for you to reach your goals."

> ♋
> *You can never let down your guard, and the best way to stay alert is to always look for ways to serve your customers better—that is, by always looking for ways to improve.*
> ♋

"Pepe, put down in your Chronicles, 'I must always strive to do better.' That will help you keep a sharp competitive focus. Also, Pepe, you must realize there are competitors who also offer similar products. They are out to expand their business, just as we are at the House of Pesce. Therefore, they will attempt to obtain business from some of the merchants with whom we do business. You can never let down your guard, and the best way to stay alert is to always look for ways to serve your customers better—that is, by always looking for ways to improve. Do you understand this lesson and the value it has on your development?"

"*Si*, Grandfather. I will remember to always look for ways to improve. I understand. I will make comments about the importance of continual improvement in my Chronicles."

Key Points in My Chronicles

⊖ I will always strive to do better. Continual improvement is a sure sign of a sales master.

⊖ Obstacles are only what I see when I take my mind off my goals.

⊖ A simple goal achievement program is the following: Decide what I want. Decide what I am willing to give up to get it. Act!

⊖ I will move ahead by eliminating those undesirable things which stand in my way.

⊖ I will ask for the business and not hesitate to answer customer concerns and objections.

CHAPTER 16

Dinner After the Show

Sharing Your Talents and
Blessings with Others

incenzo's dance company held its final show on Saturday. It had been an overwhelming success, with standing ovations at each performance. I joined my grandfather and uncle at the afternoon finale. The women in the family were at *Nonna*'s house getting ready for the dinner we would have after the show.

Grandfather, being a significant patron and contributor to the arts—particularly local artists—was elated with the activities of the Florence Dance Company. The final week's performance had been an outstanding success. He was particularly proud of his grandson and namesake, Vincenzo. All of us were proud—we all loved him.

On the way to the theater, Grandfather mentioned that he was also very proud of *Professore* Victorio Carlobutti, the artistic director of the dance company. The professor, in the period of only two years, had raised the company from near extinction to one of the finest dance companies in the entire north of Italy.

Grandfather had taken a chance when, as chairman of the artistic director selection committee, he recommended hiring the professor. Grandfather said he took the chance because he believed that the *professore* had repented for his past mistakes. When questioned by Uncle Giovanni about the initial hesitancy in hiring the professor, Grandfather related the circumstances that led to the professor being released as the artistic director of *Teatro de la Scala* in Milano. It was said that the professor had engaged in an adulterous affair with the prima ballerina, a *signorette d'ennette*.

> ೞ
> **With
> God-given
> abilities and
> proper
> training, all can
> improve.**
> ೞ

Professore Carlobutti's wife, who was a distant cousin of Cardinal Graziadei, demanded that the ballerina's agreement be terminated. The cardinal intervened and exerted pressure on the Francesco Corbani family, who were the principal benefactors of the theatre company in Milano.

The *professore* decided to resign, recognizing that if his principal dancer were asked to leave, the company would not perform up to the high standards expected. For six months before Grandfather and the Florence Dance Company Board of Directors engaged his services, the *professore* gave private dance and piano lessons to the chubby little girls of the Milanese rich.

Grandfather said, "When I looked into *Professore* Carlobutti's eyes and he admitted he made a mistake with the ballerina, I believed him."

The *professore* did wonders for our dance company in Florence. He said that with God-given abilities and proper training, all can improve. Grandpa felt he had raised the total performance to a higher level. He deserved much of the credit for the success of this week. Papa said we were blessed to have the *professore* in Florence.

"Papa, you, too, should be congratulated for your renewed faith," chided Zio Giovanni. "You picked him up when everyone else was putting him down."

"Thank you for your kind comments, my son. I was merely trying to select the best person for the artistic directorship. I felt the *professore* was the best qualified. I believe the reason God gave me the good health and fortune to live a long life is because he wanted me to help others. It is in giving and helping others, without expecting anything in return, that I receive the greatest joy. I believe God gave us His blessings to share with others."

"May you live to be one hundred, *Papa-mia*," said Uncle Giovanni.

"*Grazie*, Giovanni, *grazie*, and you also, may you live to be one hundred. My son, I enjoy sharing with others. It is the same as when you provide your services to someone who cannot pay. Do you not do that in your profession?"

"*Si*, Papa, I frequently provide my services *pro bono*, that is, without fee. When I provide my services to those who cannot compensate me, I receive great satisfaction in return. You are right, Papa. You can never out-give the giver, and you do receive more when you give more."

> ∞
> *It is in giving and helping others, without expecting anything in return, that I receive the greatest joy. I believe God gave us His blessings to share with others.*
> ∞

We settled into our seats and enjoyed the show. It was magnificent! As I reflected on this last show, I felt that I enjoyed this performance even more than the first. I guess the disappointments after my week on the road somehow made me less attentive, although I do remember jumping up after the show and seeing everyone in the theater rise to their feet as they applauded.

Because I was more relaxed this week, I could really see the brilliance of Vincenzo's performance. I do not want to brag, but I believe he was the best dancer on stage. He was outstanding in his black and white cat costume. It was an inspiring performance. During a series of leaps, the audience started applauding in appreciation and recognition of his talent. I shouted, *"Fratello mia, fratello mia, fratello mia!"* I was overcome with pride.

After the performance, we waited for Vincenzo to change. He met us in front of the theater. We were all going over to Grandfather's house for a wonderful feast. Following us in another wagon were *Professore* and *Signora* Carlobutti. They would join us for the wonderful meal we would be enjoying that evening. Grandfather also invited *Monsignore* Mazza and *Signore* and *Signora* Caputo. *Signore* Caputo was the chief magistrate of the province. Papa had known him for over forty years.

At Grandmother's house, the women were preparing a feast. They had been busy all day. The meal would be memorable. Earlier that morning, when I went over to meet Grandpa to ride in his carriage to the theater, I could already smell the aroma of the preparations starting in the kitchen,

Grandfather and Grandmother Pesce had a wonderful home. It was the central meeting place for all family members. We would get together at least once each week, in addition to Sunday dinner. It was always a real feast. Because my mother and aunt were sisters, and they both loved my grandparents, it really made our get-togethers extra special.

Grandmother really kept the house warm and comfortable. It always looked cheerful, and my grandparents welcomed all, friends and strangers. During the week, grandfather frequently sent a messenger to tell grandmother that he was bringing a guest for dinner. He knew that grandmother always cooked plenty but, when needed, could add a few more ingredients to what she had on the hearth to feed last minute guests. One thing about an Italian kitchen, there is always plenty of food for a few more hungry mouths. Grandmother was a superb cook and host. She, like grandfather, had a terrific sense of humor. They were optimists, continually looking for the bright side of any situation. They seemed to be friends with everyone in Florence.

Grandmother had fresh cut flowers on her table everyday. On the hearth she would have a small pot of boiling water with pine needles and the petals of roses, eucalyptus, and gardenias. It was a very pleasant scent that would almost eliminate the smell of garlic when she was cooking a meal. Inside the front door was a poem that Grandmother had embroidered into a small tapestry. It was the Family Prayer. The origin of the poem was unknown; however, Grandfather thought that it was written by his parents. It was found in an old trunk taken from the Isle of Ischia after the flood. Initially, it had been written on an old piece of parchment.

A FAMILY PRAYER

Keep us close, and keep us one
In everything we face,
Through Your blessings make our home
A warm and loving place.
Fill these rooms with happiness
And help us to increase
Our willingness to give of ourselves
In friendship and in peace.
Teach us how to share our hearts
And live in sweet accord
That we may always enjoy this life
Together, thank you, Lord.

Amen.

Welcome and best wishes
from Pierina and Vincenzo J. Pesce

That day, Grandmother was orchestrating the activities with the same precision that the *professore* used when staging his production. *Zia* Catherine, Mama, and Marie Angela were all busy. The meal would be a first-class production. It would be extraordinary. It would be worthy of the House of Pesce.

Marie Angela started teasing me about the menu and what they were making, but it was not long before Mama gave me the full menu, and I took a chunk of fresh hot bread and stuck it in the gravy pot. Although Mama said it was not cooked, I could not resist. I knew in a few hours it would be perfect.

The meal was a fitting tribute to the closing of Vincenzo's show. Marie Angela was dispatched into the yard to pick the lettuce and fresh tomatoes for our *antipasto*. In the *antipasto*, in addition to a couple of varieties of lettuce and sliced tomatoes, she would add slices of red and green peppers. Of course, olives and the necessary spices would be added to the virgin olive oil and pure wine vinegar.

Grandfather was very proud of his vineyard and orchard. Starting with the remaining vines recovered from his father's orchards in Ischia, he had developed a significant orchard of fruit, nut trees, herbs and spices. His vegetables were outstanding. Following the salad, Grandmother would serve cold fish marinated in oil and garlic. *Zia* Catherine, whose family was from Naples, really enjoyed making fish dishes. She was busy preparing one of her special dishes called fruit of the sea. The *insalata de frutti di mare* had shrimp, calamari, scungilli, and clams, all bought fresh that morning. The juice of fresh lemons would be added just before serving. A dish of *Zia* Catherine's specialty with a chunk of Italian bread is wonderful. I could hardly wait.

For the pasta dish, Mama prepared one of her special marinara sauces. Mother reminded me that Marinara sauce was named by townspeople who lived near the docks in Naples. The Neapolitan fishermen, when they were out to sea, did not have any meat products to make their sauce, so they used only tomatoes, oil, garlic and spices. They would sometimes add clams or mussels if they were available. When they returned to shore and wanted a similar sauce, they explained its ingredients as those requested by "mariners," those who ply the seas. Quickly, the tomato sauce they loved became known as "marinara." Mother made it delicious.

It was a wonderful day and an ideal way to conclude my first week in sales training—by enjoying the many blessings the Lord provides.

Key Points in My Chronicles

⊖ I realize that everyone deserves another chance. I will not be too quick to criticize. I pray that I will get another chance if I ever fall short of the mark.

⊖ I will share the fruits of my labors with those less fortunate and those I love. I will remember that it is only through giving that we receive.

⊖ I will continue to emphasize the good and the positive in all situations, while minimizing the bad and the negative.

⊖ Personal growth produces rewards that I can share with others.

CHAPTER 17

$\mathcal{G}$randfather and the $\mathcal{R}$enaissance $\mathcal{C}$ouncil

Surrounding Yourself with Successful People

Grandfather was very dogmatic in his approach to better serve his merchant customers. Many years ago, he established what he called the Renaissance Council with seven individuals. *Il Magnifico Seti,* as he called them. The Magnificent Seven were chosen to grandfather maintain his leadership in the fabrics business.

The prime purpose of the council was identifying what additional actions the House of Pesce could take to keep ahead of others in the business. Grandfather wanted to maintain our position as the leading fabrics provider in the entire Republic of Florence and knew that we could not maintain a leadership position without always looking for ways to improve.

"Our competitors are not sleeping," he would say, followed by, "Others are always trying to tumble the king's castle."

The make-up of the group was very interesting. Not all the members came from the business world. In response to my question about how he selected the members of the group, Grandfather replied:

"Pepe, first, I select individuals who have integrity. They are honorable and respected in the community. I may not agree with them in many areas, but that is not a problem as long as they are men of principle. They also must have experienced life. They know what positively motivates and persuades people to act. They look deeper into a situation to probe why different individuals act in particular ways. In addition, those I select have a significant amount of influence over many people in the community; they have the pulse of what is happening. And lastly, they must be willing to respond, to answer questions, and to participate in our discussions when we get together."

> ೦ೱ
> *First, I select individuals who have integrity. They are honorable and respected in the community . . . . They know what positively motivates and persuades people to act.*
> ೦ೱ

"And, Grandfather, what are these questions?"

"Pepe, the questions are not always the same; however, I usually ask questions to learn what is happening in the city and countryside. I ask whether they have heard any negative reactions about our products or services since we last met. If they are aware of any concerns, we immediately identify a course of action to quickly rectify the concern. Next, we determine what additional products or services they, or those they meet or do business with, express an interest in. This is especially important as it relates to improving the sales master/merchant relationship. Using these basic approaches as the meeting objectives, we have uncovered many new areas. This has kept us the leader in the fabrics business and will keep the House of Pesce ahead of any competitors."

The group included many diverse members. First, there was *Signore* Bugatti, the owner of the largest sewing operation in the city. Then, there was Enrico Medici, the son of Fernando Medici, the largest banker in all of Italy. Niccolo Machiavelli was a writer and a very forward thinker. Grandfather appreciated his ideas, although they were occasionally somewhat abstract. Uncle Giovanni participated to protect Grandfather from legal problems. These problems had increased with the political changes in Florence and throughout Europe. *Signore* Giovanni Corbani, the builder, also served on the Council. He knew much of what went on in Florence, especially when new cathedrals or churches were being planned. Papa knew they would need new tapestries. *Signore* Antonio LoGerfo was the largest innkeeper in all of Italy. Grandfather preferred that all the sales apprentices and sales masters stay in *Signore* LoGerfo's inns whenever they were in the territory. *Signore* LoGerfo knew much about the countryside from his travels and visiting with his innkeepers.

> *Observations or ideas arising from the council meetings frequently were used to improve the regular operations at the House of Pesce.*

The seventh member of the Council was Nicholas Mandaro, the owner of the biggest dairy and cheese processing farm in the entire province. He had grown his farm from very humble beginnings, and Grandfather trusted his judgment. We always had an ample supply of his mozzarella, provolone, parmesan, and romano cheese in the cold locker in the cellar of our home. *Signore* Mandaro was one of my grandfather's long-time and dearest friends. Members of the Council knew of *Signore* Mandaro's wonderful disposition, so they frequently hugged him and called him *Signore Grosso Formaggio*, Mr. Big Cheese.

Observations or ideas arising from the council meetings frequently were used to improve the regular operations at the House of Pesce. During one of the meetings, many years ago, a comment made by *Signore* Bugatti later turned into a major program that Grandfather initiated, putting him years ahead of his competitors.

Grandfather said it started when Federico, the pigeon keeper, came to one of the Council meetings to report that Papa's prize pigeon had just hatched six chicks, and they all looked to be in excellent health. Federico left an assistant to tend to the chicks while he ran to the house to tell Grandfather. He said the chicks were sipping some of *Signore* Mandaro's goat milk.

Signore Bugatti heard Grandfather talking to Federico about the pigeons and mentioned it would be beneficial if Grandfather could use his prize pigeons to help deliver orders. This would save *Signore* Bugatti the trouble of having to send a horseman or wagon to the House of Pesce for goods. At first, Grandfather thought there was a problem with the service being provided by Michael LaMagna, the salesman responsible for *Signore* Bugatti.

But, *Signore* Bugatti quickly clarified the situation. He said, "No, Vincenzo, young LaMagna is doing an excellent job as your representative on my account. The problem arises when he leaves and one of my patrons comes in and selects a fabric that I have in limited supply. I must dispatch one of my people, sometimes with a wagon, to retrieve the goods. I cannot wait for Michael to make his next call before I order."

> ℭℬℰℴ
> *I will listen to the marketplace and those I respect. Their input is invaluable.*
> ℭℬℰℴ

There was no further discussion at the time. Grandfather said he would have to think about how to put one of his homing pigeons in *Signore* Bugatti's place of business. Although there would be discussions with Federico, I am sure Grandfather must have made up his mind as soon as it was mentioned. Grandfather was diligent in providing more services for his customers. He frequently said, "I will listen to the marketplace and those I respect. Their input is invaluable." He was a renaissance man.

While Grandfather was talking about his prized flock of pigeons, Enrico Medici came over and started to boast of his own prized flock. I believe that is when they decided to place a wager on whose flock was better. I never heard the outcome of the wager, but Grandfather's customers are now benefiting from the innovation that came from that meeting, the pigeon delivery system.

Key Points in My Chronicles

⊖ Without a new challenge, my potential is never fully realized. I will always look for opportunities to stretch my abilities, even if it requires a learning period.

⊖ I will associate with winners, whatever their business. They are usually good communicators and I can learn from them. I will simulate the proven, desirable traits of other sales masters.

⊖ I will always look for ways to improve the service I provide my customers. That is the best way to keep customers satisfied and buying from me rather than a competitor.

⊖ I will listen to the marketplace and those I respect. Their input is invaluable.

CHAPTER 18

The Pigeon Delivery System

Selling More by Providing Better Customer Service

Grandfather had one of the finest flocks of homing pigeons in the region. His pigeons frequently won laurels when racing against other flocks. Pigeons and business were two topics Papa loved to speak about. With Federico's and my father's assistance, Grandfather had started the pigeon delivery system years ago.

Federico was one of Grandfather's most trusted employees as well as a true friend. Grandfather had known his family for a long time. Although Federico had many tasks, his primary responsibility was maintaining the sales and delivery wagons and looking after Grandfather's pigeons. He was Grandfather's highest paid employee.

Federico always named new pigeons after key stories, places or individuals that he had read about in one of the books he borrowed from Grandfather. Federico had a very sharp mind and could read Latin and Greek manuscripts. He became disabled as a boy when he was thrown from a horse. The accident left him slightly handicapped. Grandfather had paid for his medical bills as well as for his education in the monastery.

Grandfather always surrounded himself with creative people and people of integrity. Indeed, Federico was one. He had recently been reading one of the Greek classics, so the present flock of pigeons had names such as Odyssey, Ulysses, and Troy. Grandfather had named the last hatch of birds after the mythological heroes Zeus, Mercury, Hercules and Prometheus. Their most productive female pigeon was named Penelope.

"Pepe, years ago, one of my distant customers wanted fabrics before the next week's delivery. He hired a messenger rider to send the order back to us in Florence. I reimbursed the customer for the expense of the rider. Pepe, with the added expense, there was very little profit on the sale, but it helped to keep that customer satisfied. Almost at the same time, *Signore* Bugatti suggested the possible use of the pigeons. Your father, Federico, and I discovered a system that allowed the pigeons to help in delivering orders. Although slight improvements have been made over the years, the system is pretty much as it was when your father first tried it in his territory many years ago. To encourage large customers to place orders between visits, we had to make over three hundred leather folders containing sample swatches of the ninety-six designs the House of Pesce was carrying at the time. Your mother, Marie Angela and *Zia* Catherine spent weeks cutting, marking and binding the sample swatches. Each large customer was given a leather folder with a complete set of swatches. The House of Pesce had the largest number of fabrics in Florence, as well as the most customers."

Grandfather was always looking for better ways to service his merchant customers. When a merchant could not wait for the next week's delivery, or the desired fabric was not in the sales-man's wagon, it would be handled by the carrier pigeon. My father, the first territory man to try the system, would write the order on a leather band, attach it to one of the pigeon's legs, and release the bird. Quickly, the merchants started to place their orders the same way.

"If there were many orders placed during the day, your father would write them all down using the symbols we designed for merchant and fabric requirements. The next morning, he would tie the orders in a small pouch and strap it onto the leg of one of the eight carrier pigeons he had with him. Pigeons would never be re-leased after dark. Your father's furthest stop always required the strongest pigeon to handle the greater distance. He knew each bird's strength, always saving the strongest pigeon for the longer flight. The pigeons selected for the longer flights were Archimedes, Titan and Taurus."

"Next, we started to place a small coop with two of our pigeons and a set of leg bands at each large customer's business. Each mer-chant who had a coop from the House of Pesce was given a small sack of grain for feed. Cus-tomers liked the simplicity and effectiveness of our approach. Within a few hours after a pigeon was released, it would arrive on the warehouse roof where Federico or one of his trusted assistants would remove the order from the pigeon and give the bird a special snack as a reward. They would comb its plume, check its wings and give the new arrival some fresh berries from the orchard. Then they would ready a wagon with the required fabrics. Each delivery included a fresh pigeon."

I found out that Federico never sent the same pigeon back to the customer who had released it with an order. He felt the pigeon might develop a new alliance to the merchant customer and not fly directly to the House of Pesce when released.

"With the new shipment, the driver took additional feed and leather ordering straps. The wagon driver would always clean the

> ☙
> *Customers liked the simplicity and the effectiveness of our approach. Within a few hours after a pigeon was released, it would arrive on the warehouse roof. . . . Our merchant customers were overwhelmed with this service.*
> ☙

coops, make any necessary repairs and tend to the birds. Our merchant customers were overwhelmed with this service. If we received a large order early in the week, our delivery wagon would leave for the merchant's place of business within twenty-four hours."

Federico made sure that the drivers had clean uniforms, were sober, and always thanked the customers for their business. Federico paid his drivers more than the typical wages; hence, there were not many who did not follow his rules. He emphasized that satisfied customers of the House of Pesce paid all of us.

"Customers are our real employer," he would remind his drivers.

He demanded that all wagon drivers show the respect required. More than once, he fired a driver on the spot because of a complaint from a customer. Grandfather backed Federico fully.

This special delivery service with the homing pigeons was one of the reasons the House of Pesce was such a well-regarded name in the fabrics business. When the pigeons lost some of their speed and endurance, Grandfather would retire them from the messenger service and keep them for mating. Every day, Federico would go to the warehouse roof and let out the pigeons for what he called an "exercise trip." The flock, sometimes numbering as many as thirty pigeons, would fly, usually in sight, then return for a special treat of fresh picked corn and berries.

> ☙
> **Customers are our real employer, he would remind his drivers....**
> **The best way to keep a competitor away from a customer was by providing exceptional service.**
> ☙

Grandfather was always coming up with new initiatives on how to best serve our merchant customers. First, he started leaving pigeon coops at only larger accounts. As business got better and he wanted to increase his activity with the smaller accounts, he started leaving them one pigeon coop. Now all customers, except those who only buy small quantities right off the wagon, have a House of Pesce coop. Grandfather knew that the best way to keep a competitor away from a customer was by providing exceptional service. He said that having our pigeons at the customer's shop created what he called a psychological obligation. I did not know what that meant so he explained in greater detail.

"Pepe, when someone treats you kindly, what do you feel obliged to do?"

Thinking for a minute, I responded. "Papa, when I am treated nicely, I want to return the kindness. Is that not the proper thing to do?"

"Of course, it is, my son, and by wanting to return the kindness, you feel you have a debt that should be repaid as quickly as you can. I call that unreturned act of kindness a psychological obligation. The pigeons, although eating our feed, are sitting at the customer's place of business, ready to serve the customer. They place a psychological obligation on the customer who wants to return our kindness. Every day, as the merchant goes over to feed our pigeons with the small bag of feed we provide, he will think that he should 'send the pigeon home' by writing an order and sending the bird out to flight. All he has to do to relieve himself of this psychological obligation is simply to write down the fabric number and how much he wants and release the bird. Depending on the distance, the happy bird will land at our warehouse in anywhere from a few minutes to a few hours."

> ◆
> *Having our pigeons at the customer's shop created what he called a psychological obligation . . . .*
> **All he has to do to relieve himself of this psychological obligation is simply to write down the fabric number and how much he wants and release the bird.**
> ◆

Grandfather also thought that by having at least one pigeon at most of our customers, the territory salesman would have to go there to take additional feed. This was another opportunity to check the merchant for business, show any new fabrics, and update the sample inventory. It was also a good way to force the salesman to visit each customer. It was a discipline tool for the territory salesman.

Grandfather said that the first year he initiated the pigeon order system, we received about one order in twenty "that flew in," as he called it. The second year it was three in twenty. Now after so many years, almost half the orders we received are orders that fly in. Papa was a very creative person. It is no wonder that he was successful and built the House of Pesce into the largest fabric house in the entire Republic of Florence. He listened to his customers.

Grandfather had a simple philosophy about building the business: "Always look for additional ways to satisfy the customer. Do not be discouraged if everything you try does not interest every customer. Keep trying and be positive."

It seemed that many of the approaches for success as a sales apprentice I had been hearing from him, *Monsignore* Mazza, Rabbi Santucci, Uncle Giovanni, and others were not very complicated. I knew that my success would come from doing the essentials correctly.

Maybe I was looking for some magical words to say when meeting a customer— words that would assure me of instant acceptance and business, yet there is no magic involved. The essentials started to become clearer as I continued to write actions for success in my Chronicles. Sincerity, honesty, and an interest in providing quality merchandise were the real ingredients for success. It was not magic. It was hard work supported by a positive attitude.

> ༺༻
> *Sincerity, honesty, and an interest in providing quality merchandise were the real ingredients for success. It was not magic. It was hard work, supported by a positive attitude.*
> ༺༻

In looking at my Chronicles, it appeared that more and more entries addressed attitudes. That was very refreshing, because while it would take me a longer period of time to assemble knowledge about our fabrics and the skills necessary to communicate this knowledge, I had the ability to change and improve my attitudes in a fraction of a second. This discovery gave me renewed confidence that I would be successful as a sales apprentice.

Key Points in My Chronicles

⊖   I will never be totally satisfied with the way I serve my customers. I will always be open to new ideas, looking for ways to improve the quality of my products and service.

⊖   I will increase the value that I provide by being a business resource for my customers. My knowledge and expertise will give them a reason to want to see me.

⊖   I will keep competition out by providing the most value. I will build a wall around each customer based on proven performance.

⊖   I will remember that my best customers are my competition's best prospects. I must stay alert and correct any problems quickly. I will take steps to prevent problems from happening again.

⊖   Change is inevitable. People who fear change do not stretch their imagination and activities. I will view change as an opportunity to grow.

⊖   By always being sincere with my customers, they will trust me and want to do business with me.

⊖   I will do more than is expected. If the customer asks for bread, I will give him cake.

⊖   I will have sincere empathy for my customers. I will look at the situation through their eyes.

CHAPTER 19

First Trip into the Territory Since Training Started

Probing, Listening and Other Skills Get Orders

LaMagna XLIV
Rocco XXVIII
Pesce XXIV
Verde XXIII

After a week in Florence undergoing my initial salesmanship training, I thought it was time for me to go into the territory, at least for a few days. Although I could have gone out the week before with one of the reserve wagons, the time spent in training was extremely helpful. My wagon was completely repaired and refurbished. Federico had one of his assistants repaint the wheels and buckboard and reupholster the seat with a nice, new fabric. On the canvas covering, the House of Pesce name and our symbol, a fish inside a circle, was freshly painted.

Under the wagon seat was a white wooden storage area. In large, red script letters Federico had painted:

Giuseppe Pesce
Sales Professionale

Seeing the wagon gave me a very positive feeling. I was anxious to return to the field, even if only for a few days. I wanted to try the approaches mentioned by my tutors during the week and which were now written in my Chronicles. Besides, I was now totally convinced that my long-term success as a sales master would be based on my strong belief in the products and services of the House of Pesce. I wanted to apply the attitudes I possessed, particularly enthusiasm and desire, and the others that I had discussed during the last week. I was anxious to use the ideas given me by Grandfather, Uncle Giovanni, the *Monsignore*, the Rabbi, and *Signores* Bugatti and Mandaro.

> ∞
> *I really showed my discipline by making two additional calls and getting orders after I was about to quit early after a tough, unsuccessful stop.*
> ∞

My trip lasted three days. I left early on Wednesday morning and returned Friday at dusk. The results were extremely encouraging. It was a good week for this young sales apprentice. I had an opportunity to try many of the lessons I had learned. On the first day out, I effectively used the benefit ideas and the approach of the scales of balance. I persuaded one reluctant customer when I told him about our pigeon delivery system. This solved a problem of a long wait to receive orders from his present supplier, and tipped the scales in my favor.

On the second day, I really showed my discipline by making two additional calls and getting orders after I was about to quit early after a tough, unsuccessful stop. I remembered not to stop after a poor call. Also, during the entire trip I read my Chronicles.

When I returned and passed Grandfather's house, I rang my bell to be certain that he knew I was coming. Of course, when I pulled into my yard, Mama, Marie Angela, and Vincenzo were all waiting. They could tell by my face that it had been a successful trip. It was in more ways than one.

At Saturday's meeting, when Marie Angela posted my sales results, she, Grandfather, and all the other salesmen cheered. They were shouting *"Bravo! Molto bene, bravo!"* I was overcome with joy. I thanked God and my associates for their best wishes. Grandfather smiled. He was very pleased.

As I reviewed my success from the past week, I considered my plans for the coming week. Again, I would spend a few days training in Florence before heading out into the territory. I planned meetings with Papa, *Zio, Signore* Mandaro and *Signore* Bugatti. I was hoping that during my visit with *Signore* Bugatti I would see his granddaughter, Concetta Bartolommeo. I thought I might impress her with my newly found confidence. In church on Sunday, I thanked God for my renewed confidence, self-esteem and success. As if by providential intervention, the topic selected by *Monsignore* Mazza for his sermon was about using your God-given talents to the fullest. He quoted from Saint Matthew. The *Monsignore* said that when the Bible was written, the talent was a coin, and an individual's wealth could be measured, based on the number of talents they possessed. Now, although the talent is no longer the coin of the realm, the word *talent* primarily means the ability or proficiency of an individual.

> ∞
> *God would never put us into a situation without giving us the talents necessary to have it turn out successfully, although for a period of time the challenge may appear to be more than we can handle.*
> ∞

The *Monsignore* said that God, as a gift to show His goodness, blesses each of us with certain talents. It is up to us to use these gifts by multiplying them and sharing them with others. He looked at me as he said, "God would never put us into a situation without giving us the talents necessary to have it turn out successfully, although for a period of time the challenge may appear to be more than we can handle."

During the service the choir seemed particularly enthusiastic as they sang about receiving all we need from God if at first we seek His kingdom.

I left the church believing that I would develop into an outstanding sales master. Of this I was certain.

Key Points in My Chronicles

- ⊖ By using proven salesmanship skills I will be successful. I will not be discouraged if my success does not come as quickly as I would like.

- ⊖ If I feel discouraged, I will review past successes. What I accomplished before, I will accomplish again.

- ⊖ I will learn from my mistakes and strive to eliminate them by reviewing my successful experiences.

- ⊖ My positive self-image gives me confidence and credibility with customers. I will look, act, and talk like a winner. Customers want to buy from winners.

- ⊖ God blessed me with certain unique talents. I honor Him when I use them to the fullest. I will thank Him for these blessings. I will give credit and thanks where it is due.

CHAPTER 20

$\mathcal{G}$randfather $\mathcal{C}$overs $\mathcal{A}$dditional $\mathcal{S}$alesmanship $\mathcal{T}$raits

Believing in Yourself, Staying Motivated, Being Positive

efore heading back into the territory that week, I stopped in to see Grandfather.

"Giuseppe, although you are still a young man, you possess much talent. You are progressing very quickly on your journey as a sales apprentice. One area where there is little disagreement from any of my business associates is this: if you want to succeed you must have a strong belief in yourself. With a personal belief and by taking the actions listed in your Chronicles, you will be successful. The desire to succeed must be continuous, not a

125

destination where, once you have arrived, you are satisfied. Rather, success is a continuous journey. Your journey never ends after one goal is achieved. It must be followed by another one of greater challenge."

"Pepe, personal and professional growth is a dynamic challenge that requires your commitment," Grandfather continued. "It is a twenty-four-hour-a-day commitment. Remember, in providing the products and services of the House of Pesce, we are committed to serving our customers."

While he took a breath, I had a chance to ask a question about growing the business. "Papa, how do we expand our business?"

> ❦
>
> *Time and energy invested in your personal development is seed money.*
> *It must be planted today if you are to reap rewards in the future . . . .*
> *You cannot reap if you do not sow.*
>
> ❦

"Pepe, to expand our business we must develop and build by maintaining a strong relationship with our established customers while continually looking for new opportunities with prospective 'buyers.' Never forget that before selling our products and services, you must first sell yourself."

"Uncle Giovanni also mentioned selling yourself."

"*Si*, prospective customers must first 'buy' you, based on the sincerity of your approach and your helpfulness. After they are comfortable with you, then they may consider buying your products and services. Pepe, we are actually in the people business. People buying from people with our products and services as the medium. If a customer believes you, he will believe in the products and services you provide."

I asked what else I must do to grow as a sales master.

"Pepe, to perform as a professional salesman, it is essential that you continually look for ways to grow. You grow by seeking every opportunity to improve your sales knowledge, your sales skills, your sales techniques and your sales attitudes."

"This is exactly what the *Monsignore* said!"

"*Si*," continued Grandfather, "time and energy invested in your personal development is seed money. It must be planted today if you are to reap rewards in the future. It is a law of nature:

you will not see results if you do not initiate action. You cannot reap if you do not sow. You cannot enjoy the positive effects and benefits if you are not part of the cause to make it happen. The abundant harvest the House of Pesce has enjoyed in the form of recognition, income, satisfaction, peace, happiness, and success is in direct proportion to the effort our family has exerted and the seeds we have planted. Plant, and you will reach a high level of success, Pepe. Of this I am positive. If you perform professionally and are motivated and believe, you will succeed. You become motivated by challenging yourself to set ambitious goals and achieving them. Then you must set higher levels of performance. Selling is persuading a prospective customer to accept what you are offering, to believe in what you believe. You cannot persuade another to believe until you 'sell' or believe yourself. The Bible says 'All things are possible to those that believe,' and I know you believe in the Bible."

Taking a brief break, Grandfather and I shared some grapes, bread and cheese, and then Grandfather continued, "Achieving personal and professional success is never an accident, nor is it a stroke of luck confined only to a favored few. Rather, it is the inevitable result of persistent self-motivation and belief."

"Pepe, as you start your business career, make your commitment to grow through self-motivation. Prepare and read your Chronicles. Your only prerequisite is desire and a strong belief in yourself. Start by setting ambitious goals. You probably have already visualized the rewards of increased success. Act now because you do not have unlimited time to achieve your goals. Time moves on. The time to begin is not tomorrow or next week—the time to start is now! Your mental commitment is all that is required. Do not worry about what happened yesterday. That is history. You cannot change it, but you must learn from it. If there were some failures, then you have gained experience. It is what you do and

> *You become motivated by challenging yourself to set ambitious goals and achieving them. Then you must set higher levels of performance. Selling is persuading a prospective customer to accept what you are offering, to believe in what you believe.*

where you go from here that is important. It is your future, and that is where you will spend the rest of your life. Make it the best that it can be!

"Even when you are self-motivated, occasionally there may be times of indecision or doubt. There will be times when you feel you have set impossible goals and you want to give up. If that occurs, reject the negative thought and keep going. Remember that many of the greatest accomplishments of all time have been attained by men and women who, judged by normal standards, did not have a chance of succeeding. For example, Demosthenes stuttered, yet he became an outstanding orator. It was Demosthenes who said, 'small opportunities are often the beginning of great enterprises.' A few years ago, Cristopher Columbus drew an imaginary chart of an imaginary sea, and although the Italian government would not subsidize his explorations, he was not discouraged. He went to Spain and the Spanish government listened and supported him. He sailed and discovered the New World. Both men accomplished the impossible, or rather, they accomplished what most people thought was impossible. They had one thing in common—a strong belief that the world had a need for their services and talents. They had the perseverance to deliver despite handicaps. So can you, starting now!

> ☙❧
>
> *The primary benefit of a strong belief focus is the elimination of indecisiveness and fear. . . . negative thinking has no place in the confident, believing mind and attitude of a professional sales master.*
>
> ☙❧

"The primary benefit of a strong belief focus is the elimination of indecisiveness and fear. We know that negative thinking has no place in the confident, believing mind and attitude of a professional sales master. Pepe, never consider or accept defeat. You motivate yourself by your unswerving belief in your abilities, capacities, and potential. It is this self-generated belief that makes you a professional. This belief does not assure that you will succeed in every attempt. However, with a strong belief you will never accept a temporary setback as final, but recognize that it gets you closer to success. Your belief keeps you striving for a goal that you visualize. You will reach it. The man who believes he can accomplish much is correct, and so is the man who believes he cannot.

"If a customer, or others, discourage you during the day, it is essential to counterattack any negatives with positive actions. When you see someone smile and laugh, it makes you cheerful. If you run into a sad person, it makes you feel sad. These are examples of the power of suggestion—a powerful psychological force.

"It is necessary that you remain positive and self-motivated. When you project a positive attitude and self-image, others around you reflect the same. If you encounter negative people and suggestions during the day, do not allow these negatives to remain. Replace all negatives with positives. By repeating positive affirmations throughout the day, you place in your subconscious mind the stimulus to overcome temporary setbacks while keeping yourself focused. One example of a positive affirmation you should repeat during the day is 'Every day, in every way, through the grace of God, I am getting better and better.' Pepe, I have talked much; however, it was an important message and I wanted to pass it on to you. You are anxious to get into the territory. Go, have a great trip. *Arrivederci.*"

"*Grazie*, Papa. *Arrivederci.*"

Key Points in My Chronicles

- ⊖ Before I attempt to sell anything to a customer, I must first sell myself. If I do not believe that what I offer is the best total value, how can I expect the customer to believe it?

- ⊖ I know that selling is getting the customer to believe in what I believe. All things are possible to those who believe.

- ⊖ The sale starts in my mind. Therefore, I will think positive thoughts, take positive steps, and expect positive results.

- ⊖ Motivation comes from within. Self-motivation is the only true driving force. While I cannot change many situations, I have complete control over my actions.

- ⊖ I will dream of lofty goals. It is the force that drives me to higher ground.

CHAPTER 21

My Second Trip into the Territory

Getting Customers to Realize the Benefits of Ownership

LaMagna XLVI
Pesce XXXIII
Verde XXIX
Rocco XXIX

On my second trip, my results were very positive and an improvement over the previous week. I paid particular attention to my approach and used some of the techniques mentioned by Uncle Giovanni and *Signore* Mandaro. It was also special because Grandfather joined me, and we made a few calls together. Grandfather came out with the delivery wagon, and we met in the town of Prato on Wednesday. He returned with me on Friday evening. When planning the trip, I made certain to schedule stops at a few tough customers. In addition, Grandfather wanted to visit a few of his old friends. We accomplished all that we had expected.

On a few occasions, when a merchant customer was hesitant, I recalled the "value and benefits" approach and discussed the many advantages of doing business with the House of Pesce. I was able to convince two merchants and received a small order from each. It was a start with these customers—the results would get better. Grandfather convinced four additional customers, and I observed his approach. It was magnificent. With each negative comment or concern made by the customer, Grandfather listened and then repeated his understanding of the concern before making any response. His response was soft-spoken, clear, and always filled with the value to the customer. Grandfather always made sure the customer had one of our fine fabrics in his hands. With one customer, he talked about the shine and smoothness of the silk as the customer rubbed the cloth. With another, he talked about the brilliance of the colors; and with yet another, he described the weaving process that gave the cloth its strength. Each time he conducted these demonstrations, he made sure that the customer had a sample of the fabric in his hands. Later, Papa said that this made the customer actually feel and see the benefits of ownership. Another thing he always did was to convince the customer that the final product made from our fabric, whether it be a garment, a furniture covering, a tapestry or a church ornament, would be one of which the customer could be proud. I know that Grandfather was very successful as a sales master because he sincerely believed that the products and services he provided were the best available. Thursday, at the end of a very successful day, Grandfather said he wanted to take me to a special place.

> *With each negative comment or concern made by the customer, Grandfather listened and then repeated his understanding of the concern before making any response.*

"Pepe, this was my favorite swimming stream. I remember talking about it with your father. He also enjoyed its cool waters. Let us take off our tunics and go in for a refreshing swim—we earned the pleasure. Pepe, always take the time to exercise and refresh yourself after a fruitful day. Your concern must be that you do not quit early because you are frustrated by poor calls.

When you are undisciplined, and without a positive focus, it is easy to stop for the day to avoid additional frustration. That is exactly when you must make additional calls. Never end the day with an unsuccessful call. Stop only after you have achieved your objectives for the day.

"Come, Pepe, let us now relax and enjoy the daylight hour before dinner by taking a refreshing swim."

After the swim and dinner, we reviewed the activities of the day by going over my brief notes. During the day, after each call, we would go over what had been discussed, my approach, and my sales techniques. Grandfather made comments and suggestions as necessary. He is a master trainer. Although record keeping is time-consuming, and many of the salesmen working for Grandfather do not like what they refer to as "paper work," they all know that it helps them keep track of their actions. They say it forces them to be organized, particularly when they have a large number of customers. At that time, I had thirty-six customers. In time, I would have over one hundred customers, and I wanted to start with a disciplined approach.

One of the many things I have learned from my training is that a "no" is not a personal rejection. It just means that I did not use my skills to the fullest or that I was not prepared to respond as well as I could have. Both situations could be addressed with training and practice. I could always go back to those who did not buy when I become more proficient. I recognize that a "no" is not necessarily a permanent rejection, but only a temporary delay because I did not create enough interest. This gives me an opportunity to try again. My trip with Grandfather was wonderful; he helped me in so many ways.

> ∞
> *Although record keeping is time consuming and many of the salesmen working for Grandfather do not like what they refer to as "paper work," they all know that it helps them keep track of their actions.*
> ∞

Key Points in My Chronicles

⊖ An initial rejection does not mean the customer is lost. I may lose one order, but I can always go back to discuss something new or attempt a different approach.

⊖ I will get the customer involved in my demonstration by letting them sense the value of ownership. I will let them feel the quality of my products.

⊖ I must learn, think about, and apply proven sales skills to be successful. Practice does not make perfect unless what I practice is right.

⊖ Recording my customers' activities pays dividends. It is my reference for future actions and a tool for measuring my improvement.

⊖ Real salesmanship begins when a customer says "no." Sales masters work at handling the tough situations that the failures give up on.

⊖ I will analyze and understand why the customer said "yes" *and* why the customer said "no." Knowing the real and honest reason why I earned the order may be as meaningful in the long run as learning why I lost an order.

CHAPTER 22

$\mathscr{G}$randfather $\mathcal{T}$alks About $\mathscr{S}$elf-$\mathscr{D}$iscipline

Managing Your Time, Your Emotions, and Your Actions

"Giuseppe, although I have talked about some of these areas before, they are so important I will go over a few again. The primary reason most salespeople fail at being successful in sales is they lack discipline."

"Lack discipline, Papa? You mean they do not do what they are told? Like when *Mama mia* used to correct Marie Angela, Vincenzo, and me when we were younger and did not listen to her? 'Be careful with the axe,' she would say when we chopped wood for the stove, or 'Watch out for the thorns,' when we went into the woods to pick berries and, 'Be careful when you ride the horse and jump over the walls.' Papa, Mother always said she disciplined us because she loved us and wanted no harm to come to us. How does the lack of discipline cause salespeople harm?"

"Well, Pepe, I will talk about the positive aspects of discipline that can help you become successful. When we review them, it will become obvious how the lack of discipline will be harmful. I prefer the positive approach. Giuseppe, discipline to a sales apprentice means many things. Take out your Chronicles and write down the key ideas as we discuss them, one at a time."

As I removed the Chronicles from my satchel, Grandfather began.

> ∞
> *Discipline to a sales apprentice means many things. . . . First, it means having an objective. It is essential you have a destination and a goal. . . . Discipline also means that you must have a specific purpose for each customer you call on.*
> ∞

"First, it means having an objective. What do you want to achieve? It is essential that you have a destination and a goal."

"Papa, does that mean seeing all the merchant customers on the route on my weekly trip?"

"*Si*, Pepe, seeing all those on your schedule is an important part of being disciplined. However, it is essential to go deeper than that. To see all your customers is based on how disciplined and efficient you are in your stops— the time you start in the morning and the time you quit in the evening. Consider the time it takes to bridle your horse and ready your samples. These are all important, because the more proficient you become, the more time you will have available to see new prospective customers. Pepe, did *Zio* Giovanni talk to you about calling on new customers and tipping the scales in your favor? Like a lever? What you want is leverage with your customers. Although Giovanni is not a sales master, he is always anxious to talk about how to get others to look favorably on his ideas. He is a peddler lawyer, selling opinions. That is his legal training. Ha, ha, my son Giovanni, the peddler *avvocato*."

"*Si*, Papa, Uncle Giovanni did talk about leverage and the scales."

"Pepe, discipline also means that you must have a specific fabric, approach, and purpose for each customer you call on. The difference between being a successful sales apprentice and just a commercial visitor is that the salesman makes sure his purpose is clearly directed at getting an agreement and receiving an order for goods. Do you follow me so far, my son?"

"*Si*, Papa. Please go on."

"Pepe, discipline also means that you must be resilient and be able to bounce back if a customer makes an undesirable comment or objects to your offering. You cannot let a negative comment, or the actions of one merchant, affect your performance for the remainder of the day—or even worse, for the remainder of your route. Negative remarks from one customer must be thrown out of your mind as you approach the next customer with a positive demeanor. Giuseppe, you grow as a sales apprentice by learning how to handle opposition to your offerings. This is also discipline. The opposition you face strengthens you, just as the heat from the furnace makes the horseshoe pliable so it can be shaped. When it is cooled it becomes tougher than it was before."

> ଔୠ
> *Frequently, in the customer's objection, you will actually identify the real concern and address it promptly. The best approach . . . is to listen and never argue.*
> ଔୠ

"Papa, when I am in the territory it sometimes feels like I am in the furnace, particularly when a customer objects to my offering and opposes my approach. This, I am sorry to admit, Grandfather, is when I sometimes become defensive and frustrated and have to keep myself from becoming bitter. How can I turn that opposition into a positive situation?"

"Pepe, by understanding why a customer opposes your approach you become better prepared and more resilient for the next opportunity. You will learn how to respond better. You will be more comfortable after you have heard and satisfactorily responded. Frequently, in the customer's objection, you will actually identify the real concern and address it promptly. The best approach you can take, Pepe, is to listen and never argue. Then you should address their concern in a pleasant tone, always maintaining your composure. As the customer continues with his objections, you will note an opportunity to respond and present one of the many advantages the customer will enjoy when he does business with the House of Pesce. Of course, initially you may empathize with their concerns, then you balance the scales in your favor the way Uncle Giovanni suggested. Opposition from one customer better prepares you for the next stop. It helps you keep focused and disciplined. Is that clear, Pepe?"

"*Si*, Papa. Please continue."

"Giuseppe, there is also the discipline that arises during the day after you have been rejected a few times. You may think the best thing to do is to quit early. That is when you may pull your wagon off the road and take a nap, or you may look for a cool stream to take a refreshing bath, or you may decide to dig up a few worms and go fishing. All this is lost time while there are still many hours of daylight that can be better used to visit additional customers. You see, Pepe, if you quit early because of rejection, you lose in two ways."

> ***Time is one of your most cherished resources. It cannot be stored and saved for a later opportunity. It can only be used presently.***

I could not contain myself. I had to ask, "Papa, when you were in the territory, did you ever quit early and jump into a stream for a refreshing swim?"

With a big smile, Papa gave me a hug and responded, "Pepe, my Pepe, of course. When I was just starting my career as a sales apprentice it seems I spent so much time in the water I was becoming quite an accomplished swimmer." He laughed then continued, "Your grandmother could tell if I had a good week or a poor week simply by looking at the amount of soiled clothes I brought back at the end of the trip. If I had a good week, there were several soiled clothes, but if I had a bad week, she knew I spent much time in the water, because I did not have many soiled clothes. I washed them as I swam."

He saw my questioning look as I asked, "How else do you lose?"

"Secondly, you lose because you have wasted that time—time that could have been spent in front of a prospect. Pepe, time is one of your most cherished resources. It cannot be stored and saved for a later opportunity. It can only be used presently. The best way to maximize the time available is to use it as productively as possible. Pepe, one more thing about water holes. Your beloved father and I frequently compared locations where we stopped. He knew even more stops than I did, God bless his soul. When you go home, ask your mother if she ever used the soiled clothes to determine if your father had a good trip in the field."

"Pepe, it is not unusual to feel discouraged after disappointments and rejections. It means that you have to try harder, be more creative, bounce back. That is where discipline comes in. It is your ability to keep focused and keep moving ahead. Do you see the value of discipline as an important characteristic for success as a sales apprentice?"

"*Si*, Grandfather, it is very important, I will enter it in my Chronicles."

> ⋙
> *It is not unusual to feel discouraged after disappointments and rejections. It means that you have to try harder, be more creative, bounce back. That is where discipline comes in.*
> ⋘

Key Points in My Chronicles

—————— ⊰⊱ ——————

⊖ I realize that self-discipline is essential for a sales master. I will be organized and do all the important things necessary to maintain control of my time and other resources.

⊖ The best time to overcome customer objections is before they occur. My presentation should cover enough benefits that objections are few. When they are raised, I will present additional values.

⊖ I will respond to objections positively and present the advantages of what I provide.

⊖ I will have definite, *measurable* sales objectives for each call. After each call I will ask myself, "Did I achieve my objectives for this call? If not, why not?"

⊖ I will never stop for the day after a poor call. Instead, I will make another call so that I always end on a positive call.

CHAPTER 23

$\mathcal{D}$iscussing $\mathcal{E}$thics

A Professional Never Compromises Integrity

had another good week in the territory. There had been many over the last few months, and it was wonderful reporting my results at the Saturday sales meetings. My increased knowledge about what it took to flourish as a sales apprentice gave me the confidence to ask for more orders and get them.

In particular, I experienced the positive results that occur when I approached each customer with an unshakable belief in the complete package I delivered. I was convinced that my fabrics and services, backed by the House of Pesce and supported by my commitment as the territory salesman, were absolutely the best for the customer. Of course, my believing this package was the best for the customer was only the beginning. It was my challenge to get the customer to believe in the same thing.

After Saturday's meeting, I wanted to talk to grandfather about something I was told by another traveling salesman, Rosario. I had been thinking of my discussion with Rosario for days, and I could not wait to get grandfather's opinion of one of the comments he made.

During the week, while eating at an inn in Lucca, Rosario joined me at my table. He said that he sold leather goods, including pouches, purses, sandals, and boots. Rosario had been on the road for over five years and was very successful. I told him I was just starting out as a territory salesman.

I thought I could learn some valuable information to put in my Chronicles, so I asked him several questions about selling. Most of the points he made reinforced the ideas and approaches that grandfather, Uncle Giovanni, and my other tutors discussed with me. Except one. This is what I wanted to talk to grandfather about. Rosario told me that talking merchants into buying products they do not need, or want, is how he makes most of his earnings. He went on to say that even if a merchant does not have customers who would buy leather goods, Rosario would still try to pressure him into buying.

I was shocked and thought this was not proper. Selling products that a customer does not require seems unethical, or at least unprofessional. I wanted to talk to grandfather and get his feelings about this type of sales tactic. I could not wait for the opportunity, which would be after our Saturday sales meeting.

After Marie Angela tallied all the numbers reported by the salesmen and the accounts from Federico's pigeon orders, she said with a big smile that this was the most fabrics ever sold in one week. It was a record! It was a joyous sales meeting. At the end of the meeting, I approached grandfather.

"Papa, is it proper to sell fabrics to a customer even if it is not right for them?" I caught Papa by surprise, because he was still thinking about the excellent sales results.

"What did you say, Pepe?"

"Papa, last week I met a sales master who sells leather products for a manufacturer in Pisa. He says he obtains many orders by persuading people to buy his products even if they are not needed or wanted. Papa, I do not do this, I think it is unethical!"

"Pepe, you are referring to a situation where a merchant has no need or want for our fabrics and not a mere objection to buying from you. Yes, it is a question of ethics."

"Papa, I know that if a merchant uses fabrics in his business, then there is a need, and if they mention an objection or concern, I will still pursue the business and try to get an order. Over the last few months, in those situations, I have been using the approaches that I have learned in my training. They are all recorded in my Chronicles, and I review them daily. The results, you have noted, show my progress."

"Giuseppe, the progress you have shown is a testament to your desire to be successful. You are always in my prayers and they have been answered. I built this business by developing a long-term relationship with each of our customers. As you know, there are many customers who have been buying from us since we started in business over thirty years ago. This long-term success with customers is something we have earned because we have their trust and they believe in us. We have grown because we are committed to helping our merchant customers grow their business by using the House of Pesce fabrics.

> ❦
> *This long-term success with customers is something we have earned because we have their trust and they believe in us. We have grown because we are committed to helping our merchant customers grow their business.*
> ❦

"My son, there are three reasons I do not want you to ever sell fabrics to those who have no need, interest, or want. The first is pure economics. You will lose that customer. Pepe, if you talk fast and finally persuade a person to buy, even if they have no need or want, you may get one sale, but that is all. As soon as the person realizes that they were hoodwinked and taken advantage of, they will not buy again. The situation is economic because you exchange a long-term relationship, which could have possibly meant hundreds of sales, for a one-time sale. The second is also an economic reason. You will lose other customers. A dissatisfied customer will tell many people they know that you, and the company you represent, are unethical and not trustworthy. It is impossible to calculate how much we can lose because of a poor relationship with even one customer.

"The third reason is based on ethics. Pepe, I do not want you to ever pressure anyone to buy if it is not in their best interest. If there is ever any question as to the approach you should take, look into a mirror and ask yourself, 'Will my products and services benefit the customer?' If the answer is 'no,' or if you are unsure, then do not sell it until you do know, or the answer is 'yes.' Is that clear enough, Giuseppe?"

"Very clear, Grandfather, very clear. I will go home now. Marie Angela, Vincenzo, and I told Mama that we will prepare a picnic lunch and go to the River Arno for an outing." Grandfather was very pleased that we were spending time with our mother.

"*Bene* Pepe. *Molto bene.* Give my love to your mother, Vincenzo, and Marie Angela. *Arrivederci.*"

Key Points in My Chronicles

⊖   Never sell your integrity. The happiness of your life is in direct relationship to the character of your thoughts. Never be unethical.

⊖   Do not forsake your long-term benefit for a short-term profit. Life is a self-fulfilling prophecy; you usually get what you expect. Think and plan great things if you want them to happen.

⊖   Remember to enjoy your success with others because your rewards will be in direct proportion to what you give. To get more, you must give more.

⊖   I will try to put myself in my customer's place. If I were the customer, would I buy my products from me?

CHAPTER 24

*C*onclusion

A Review of a Few Key Points and a Reminder to Never Stop Learning

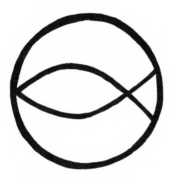

It had been some time since I started my training as a sales master, and the improvements had been significant. Still there was much to learn.

I learned the importance of continually staying in a positive frame of mind. Without my faith in God, I know this would have been difficult because of the rejections that can attack my focus and drive. I learned that my strong belief and positive conviction in what I do and who I represent make it easier to endure any hardship.

I have found that the key summary points recorded in my Chronicles are an excellent source of reference. They remind me of the situations discussed with my many mentors and the proper actions to take.

Grandfather suggested that I prepare a Salesperson's Credo, which I did, and I will end my story with it. He said a credo is what you get when you have finished thinking a thing through. It is something solid, something you can build on. I read it daily, along with my Chronicles.

I hope this story, the Chronicles, and the Salesperson's Credo help you to build a life that gives you, and all those close to you, the joys and success you desire. That is my wish.

Keep believing that the best is yet to come. It is. Have a great forever.

Giuseppe Pesce

CHAPTER 25

$\mathcal{T}$he $\mathcal{S}$alesperson's $\mathcal{C}$redo

My Daily Reminders

CB This day I will . . . prepare my samples and always be ready to present them to a prospective customer.

CB This day I will . . . encourage the customer to hold my product during the presentation. I will point out customer benefits and values.

CB This day I will . . . approach each customer with positive anticipation and enthusiasm. I will get each involved in my presentation.

CB This day I will . . . look for the best approach to show customers how our products and services will help them sell more to their customers. I will grow my business by helping others grow their business.

ఴ This day I will . . . not let a disappointment with one customer deter me from having a positive approach on the next call.

ఴ This day I will . . . approach each customer with a strong belief that I offer products and services that provide the best value.

ఴ This day I will . . . read my Chronicles and be determined to take the actions mentioned. I will be thorough, enthusiastic, and persistent.

ఴ This day I will . . . remember that all customer rejections are professional, not personal. I will brush off rejections. I will strive to improve my professionalism thereby reducing the number of rejections I hear.

ఴ This day I will . . . not stop my calling after a negative customer contact. I will end each day only after a positive call, thus I never go to sleep with negative thoughts about my abilities.

ఴ This day I will . . . not stop before I have adequately accomplished my goals for the day. I will be disciplined.

ఴ This day I will . . . remember that I will never have a shortage of money unless I have a shortage of ideas. With the right ideas I will earn enough money.

ఴ This day I will . . . repeat at least one hundred times the following self-motivator:

> *Every day, in every way, through the grace of God, I am getting better and better.*

ఴ This day I will . . . show my enthusiasm in my mannerisms and outlook. I will make all those that I meet pleased that I passed their way.

ఴ This day I will . . . recall that knowledge is not power unless I am able to clearly communicate what I know to others.

CB This day I will . . . be cautious about giving advice. Wise men do not need it, and fools will not heed it.

CB This day I will . . . resolve to listen more and talk less. No one ever learns anything by talking; it is only when one listens that one learns.

CB This day before each call I will repeat this prayer:

I believe that I am always divinely guided.

I believe I will always be led to take the right turn.

I believe that God will always make a way where there is no way.

CB This day I will . . . look to brighten the day of at least one person without expecting anything in return. I want at least one person to benefit from my passing his way.

CB This day I will . . . be passionate in my resolve to be a sales master.

I believe that if I do all of the above today, then when I rest at night, review my accomplishments, and say my prayers of thanks, I will know that I have done my best and God will bless me. *Pace*, Peace.

Glossary
of Italian and Latin Words

A.D.	anno Domini, after death. In the year of our Lord, from the passage of Christ.
Amore	love
Antipasto	appetizer, before pasta
Arrivederci	good-bye, so long
Avvocato	lawyer, attorney
Bella mia	term of affection, my beautiful one
Bene	good, fine, very well
Buon giorno	good day
Buona notte	good night
Buona sera	good evening
Casa	house, home
Ciao	hi, hello, good-bye
Consigliere	advisor, counselor
Famiglia	family
Florins	Italian coin during the Renaissance
Formaggio	cheese
Fratello	brother
Frutta di Mare	fruit of the sea
Gesu Cristo	Jesus Christ
Gnocchi	small potato and flour dumplings, usually served with tomato sauce
Grazie	thank you
Grosso	big, large
Insalata	salad (vegetables or sea food)
Mama Mia	my mother
Marinara sauce	tomato sauce made without meat, said to be named by Italian Mariners
Mazza di fiori	bouquet

153

Mia	mine
Molto	many, several, very much
Monsignore	Monsignor, a rank between a priest and a bishop in the Catholic Church
Nonna	grandmother
Nonno	grandfather
Pace	peace
Paesano	friend, countryman
Perche	why
Primavera	fresh vegetables sauteed in a light sauce, usually served with fettuccini pasta
Professore	professor, also used to indicate a recognized authority in medicine or the arts
Regina Pacis	Queen of Peace (Mother of Christ)
Si	yes
Signor	gentleman, Mr., used when addressing the person. *Signore* used when referring to a male
Signora	lady, wife, Mrs.
Signorette d'ennette	a prima ballerina
Signorina	young lady, Miss
Teatro	theater
Zia	aunt
Zio	uncle

Roman Numerals

M	1000
D	500
C	100
L	50
X	10
V	5
I	1

154   Glossary

About The Author

Vince Pesce is an author, sales trainer, professional speaker and consultant. After receiving a degree in electrical engineering, he joined Westinghouse Electric Corporation, where he sold over $100 million in capital equipment. He won the prestigious president's club award for selling over 120 percent of sales goals for four consecutive years. Vince was selected sales manager of the year by Allis-Chalmers and later promoted to director of sales training and motivational programs for Siemens-Allis at their corporate headquarters in Atlanta.

In 1985, Vince formed Advancement Associates, a firm offering sales and customer service training. He also provides consulting services. Many of the world's most renowned companies and associations are his clients. Vince's workshops and presentations are acclaimed as outstanding for their helpfulness, enthusiasm and high degree of participation. He continues to help thousands of new and veteran sales and customer service personnel to become more successful.

Vince Pesce's best selling business book, *A Complete Manual of Professional Selling*, published by Prentice Hall, has sold tens of thousands of copies. It is used by many companies and individuals to help them achieve sales success. His articles have appeared in national magazines. Since 1976, Vince has been a professional member of the National Speakers Association. He is a founder and past president of the Georgia Speakers Association.

For further information on sales, sales management, customer service or other training programs, contact Advancement Associates at (770) 908-1492, (800) 537-3551, or by fax at (770) 908-7219.

Order Form Renaissance Selling

Fax Orders: Copy this form and fax it to: (770) 908-7219

☎ Telephone orders: Call (770) 908-1492 or Toll Free: (800) 537-3551. Have your credit card ready.

✉ Mail orders: Fish Publishing
    P.O. Box 450093 • Atlanta, Georgia 31145-0093

Please send _____ copies of *Renaissance Selling, Enduring Wisdom From The Italian Masters* (ISBN 1-887951-11-3) for $24.95 each, plus $3.00 handling for the first book and $1.00 for each additional book. Allow 15 days for delivery. Air Mail: $3.50 per book. For Georgia shipments, add applicable sales tax.

Call for discounts on ten or more copies.

Payment

My check or money order for $ _____ is enclosed.

Canadian orders must be in U.S. funds.

Please charge my:

Visa _____ MasterCard _____ American Express _____ Discover _____

Card # _____

Name on card: _____

Expiration Date _____

Ship to:

Name: _____

Organization: _____

Address: _____

City/State/Zip: _____

Telephone: _____

Fax # _____

Please make your check payable and return to:

Fish Publishing

P.O. Box 450093

Atlanta, Georgia 31145-0093